SACRED TEXTS

THE
DHAMMAPADA

The Essential Teachings of The Buddha

Translated by
Dr Friedrich Max Müller

Introduction to this edition by
Kevin Trainor PhD

WATKINS
Sharing Wisdom
Since 1893

This translation of *The Dhammapada* was first published in a
volume of Sacred Wisdom of the East in 1870

First published in 2006

This edition first published in 2016 by Watkins,
an imprint of Watkins Media Limited
Unit 11, Shepperton House
89-93 Shepperton Road
London N1 3DF

enquiries@watkinspublishing.com

5 7 9 10 8 6

Designed in Great Britain by Jerry Goldie
Typeset in Great Britain by Dorchester Typesetting Group
Printed and bound in the Great Britain by TJ Books Ltd.

Library of Congress Cataloging–in-Publication data available

ISBN: 978-1-78028-969-4

www.watkinspublishing.com

CONTENTS

CONTENTS

BIOGRAPHIES

Dr. F. Max Müller was Professor of Philology at Oxford University, and the celebrated editor of the fifty volume *Sacred Books of the East* series. At the turn of the 20th century, this series brought the most important Eastern scriptures to the notice of the Western world. Müller's translations continue to be regarded as the best, and his elegant English prose is consistently faithful to the original Pali of the Dhammapada.

Kevin Trainor PhD is Associate Professor of Religion at the University of Vermont, and a noted authority on the life of the Buddha. He has written a number of highly regarded books on Buddhism and Buddhist architecture.

INTRODUCTION

The *Dhammapada*, a collection of 423 verses attributed to Gautama Buddha, has a venerable history, both in Asia and in the West. It was the first complete Buddhist canonical text published in Europe in a critical edition with translation (into Latin, in 1855), and it has probably been translated into English and other European languages more frequently than any other Buddhist text.

The *Dhammapada*'s importance for Asian Buddhists over the course of more than two millennia is suggested by its inclusion in the scriptural collections of several Buddhist schools. In addition to the Pali language version upon which this translation is based, similar collections survive in Sanskrit, Prakrit, Tibetan and Chinese. The Pali *Dhammapada* has long held a special status in the Sri Lankan Theravada Buddhist tradition; monks commonly commit the whole text to memory

during their monastic training and frequently base
their sermons on its verses.

The text's title, *Dhammapada*, resists simple translation. *Dhamma*, the Pali equivalent of the Sanskrit
Dharma, is one of the most important terms in Buddhist
tradition, and it bears a number of different but related
connotations. It can refer to the fundamental truth
about reality to which the Buddha awoke under the tree
of enlightenment ('Buddha' is a title meaning 'one who
has awoken'), to the words through which he taught
that truth to his followers, to the authoritative corpus
of those teachings, and finally, to the 'phenomena'
or constantly changing interdependent elements that
form our experience. All of these related senses of the
term appear in the *Dhammapada*'s first chapter: see
verse one in which 'All that we are' (*dhamma* in the
plural) is said to follow from our thoughts; verse five
where hatred's inability to end hatred is characterized
as an old 'rule' (*dhamma*, singular); and verse twenty
where mere recitation of memorized text is distinguished from living fully in accordance with the 'law'
(*dhamma*, singular) to which that text refers. *Dhamma*
in the text's title implies all of these. The term *pada* at

the end of the title likewise evokes multiple meanings: it can be translated 'path', 'verses' or 'words'. One needn't choose among these, since the *Dhammapada* is a collection of words set in verse that present the Buddha's 'middle path' to the realization of liberating truth.

The *Dhammapada* is divided into twenty-six chapters, each loosely organized around a common theme. For example, the opening chapter, 'The Twin Verses', presents ten sets of paired verses, each pair defining a set of contrasting behaviors or perspectives along with the negative or positive outcome that each brings about. Thus in the first two verses, evil thought leads to pain, while pure thought leads to happiness. In verses thirteen and fourteen, passion penetrates an unreflecting mind, while a well-reflecting mind effectively repels it. These verses, like many others in the collection, give a palpable force to abstract moral and cognitive states through the use of vivid images drawn from daily life. The plodding but inexorable progress of a bullock behind a plow, the inescapability of one's own shadow, and the inevitable leaking of a poorly thatched roof in a sudden rainstorm, bring home the verses' message and effectively connect the reader in the present day with the world of ancient India more than two millennia ago.

There is as well much in this text that reminds us of its distance from us. The world of the *Dhammapada* is inhabited by powerful *devas* or gods who live in an ascending hierarchy of celestial realms. Unlike the eternal creator God found in the Jewish and Christian Bibles, these gods are ultimately subject to death and rebirth. Prominent among them is Mara, the embodiment of death and the endless round of rebirths, who serves as the Buddha's nemesis.

Yellow-robed mendicants are also frequently at hand: all the verses in the collection's penultimate chapter center on the exemplary qualities and accomplishments of *bhikshus*, ordained members of the Buddhist monastic community. The verses celebrate their self-control and utter detachment from sensual pleasures, along with their independence. At the same time, their beneficent effect on those around them comes through, as in verse 382, where a young monk who applies himself to the Buddha's teaching 'brightens up this world, like the moon when freed from clouds'.

[4]

Finally, a brief note about the translator, Friedrich Max Müller, who produced the first complete English translation of the *Dhammapada*. He was a towering figure in the world of nineteenth-century scholarship on India and the religions of Asia, and is considered one of the founders of the modern discipline of comparative religion. Convinced that a systematic and rigorous comparison of the world's diverse religious traditions would provide the foundation for a true form of religion, he translated numerous Indian religious texts, and edited the monumental *Sacred Books of the East*, in which this translation appeared.

Kevin Trainor

The University of Vermont

CHAPTER I

THE TWIN-VERSES

1 All that we are is the result of what we have thought: it is founded on our thoughts, it is made up of our thoughts. If a man speaks or acts with an evil thought, pain follows him, as the wheel follows the foot of the ox that draws the carriage.

2 All that we are is the result of what we have thought: it is founded on our thoughts, it is made up of our thoughts. If a man speaks or acts with a pure thought, happiness follows him, like a shadow that never leaves him.

3 'He abused me, he beat me, he defeated me, he robbed me,'—in those who harbour such thoughts hatred will never cease.

4 'He abused me, he beat me, he defeated me, he robbed me,'—in those who do not harbour such thoughts hatred will cease.

5 For hatred does not cease by hatred at any time: hatred ceases by love, this is an old rule.

6 The world does not know that we must all come to an end here;—but those who know it, their quarrels cease at once.

7 He who lives looking for pleasures only, his senses uncontrolled, immoderate in his food, idle, and weak, Mâra (the tempter) will certainly overthrow him, as the wind throws down a weak tree.

8 He who lives without looking for pleasures, his senses well controlled, moderate in his food, faithful and strong, him Mâra will certainly not overthrow, any more than the wind throws down a rocky mountain.

9 He who wishes to put on the yellow dress without having cleansed himself from sin, who disregards also temperance and truth, is unworthy of the yellow dress.

10 But he who has cleansed himself from sin, is well grounded in all virtues, and endowed also with temperance and truth, he is indeed worthy of the yellow dress.

11 They who imagine truth in untruth, and see untruth in truth, never arrive at truth, but follow vain desires.

12 They who know truth in truth, and untruth in untruth, arrive at truth, and follow true desires.

13 As rain breaks through an ill-thatched house, passion will break through an unreflecting mind.

14 As rain does not break through a well-thatched house, passion will not break through a well-reflecting mind.

15 The evil-doer mourns in this world, and he mourns in the next; he mourns in both. He mourns and suffers when he sees the evil (result) of his own work.

16 The virtuous man delights in this world, and he delights in the next; he delights in both. He delights and rejoices, when he sees the purity of his own work.

17 The evil-doer suffers in this world, and he suffers in the next; he suffers in both. He suffers when he thinks of the evil he has done; he suffers more when going on the evil path.

18 The virtuous man is happy in this world, and
he is happy in the next; he is happy in both.
He is happy when he thinks of the good he has
done; he is still more happy when going on the
good path.

19 The thoughtless man, even if he can recite a
large portion (of the law), but is not a doer of
it, has no share in the priesthood, but is like a
cowherd counting the cows of others.

20 The follower of the law, even if he can recite
only a small portion (of the law), but, having
forsaken passion and hatred and foolishness,
possesses true knowledge and serenity of mind,
he, caring for nothing in this world or that to
come, has indeed a share in the priesthood.

CHAPTER II

ON EARNESTNESS*

21 Earnestness is the path of immortality (Nirvâna), thoughtlessness the path of death. Those who are in earnest do not die, those who are thoughtless are as if dead already.

22 Having understood this clearly, those who are advanced in earnestness delight in earnestness, and rejoice in the knowledge of the Ariyas (the elect).

23 These wise people, meditative, steady, always possessed of strong powers, attain to Nirvâna, the highest happiness.

24 If an earnest person has roused himself, if he is not forgetful, if his deeds are pure, if he acts with consideration, if he restrains himself, and lives according to law,—then his glory will increase.

25 By rousing himself, by earnestness, by restraint and control, the wise man may make for himself an island which no flood can overwhelm.

26 Fools follow after vanity, men of evil wisdom. The wise man keeps earnestness as his best jewel.

27 Follow not after vanity, nor after the enjoyment of love and lust! He who is earnest and meditative, obtains ample joy.

28 When the learned man drives away vanity by earnestness, he, the wise, climbing the terraced heights of wisdom, looks down upon the fools, free from sorrow he looks upon the sorrowing crowd, as one that stands on a mountain looks down upon them that stand upon the plain.

29 Earnest among the thoughtless, awake among the sleepers, the wise man advances like a racer, leaving behind the hack.

30 By earnestness did Maghavan (Indra) rise to the lordship of the gods. People praise earnestness; thoughtlessness is always blamed.

31 A Bhikshu (mendicant) who delights in earnestness, who looks with fear on thoughtlessness, moves about like fire, burning all his fetters, small or large.

32 A Bhikshu (mendicant) who delights in reflection, who looks with fear on thoughtlessness, cannot fall away (from his perfect state)—he is close upon Nirvâna.

CHAPTER III

THOUGIIT

33 As a fletcher makes straight his arrow, a wise
man makes straight his trembling and unsteady
thought, which is difficult to guard, difficult to
hold back,

34 As a fish taken from his watery home and thrown
on the dry ground, our thought trembles all
over in order to escape the dominion of Mâra
(the tempter).

35 It is good to tame the mind, which is difficult to
hold in and flighty, rushing wherever it listeth;
a tamed mind brings happiness.

36 Let the wise man guard his thoughts, for they
are difficult to perceive, very artful, and they
rush wherever they list: thoughts well guarded
bring happiness.

37 Those who bridle their mind which travels far, moves about alone, is without a body, and hides in the chamber (of the heart), will be free from the bonds of Mâra (the tempter).

38 If a man's faith is unsteady, if he does not know the true law, if his peace of mind is troubled, his knowledge will never be perfect.

39 If a man's thoughts are not dissipated, if his mind is not perplexed, if he has ceased to think of good or evil, then there is no fear for him while he is watchful.

40 Knowing that this body is (fragile) like a jar, and making his thought firm like a fortress, one should attack Mâra (the tempter) with the weapon of knowledge, one should watch him when conquered, and should never rest.

41 Before long, alas! this body will lie on the earth, despised, without understanding, like a useless log.

42 Whatever a hater may do to a hater, or an enemy to an enemy, a wrongly-directed mind will do him greater mischief.

43 Not a mother, not a father will do so much, nor any other relatives; a well-directed mind will do us greater service

CHAPTER IV

FLOWERS*

44 Who shall overcome this earth, and the world of Yama (the lord of the departed), and the world of the gods? Who shall find out the plainly shown path of virtue, as a clever man finds the (right) flower?

45 The disciple will overcome the earth, and the world of Yama, and the world of the gods. The disciple will find out the plainly shown path of virtue, as a clever man finds the (right) flower.

46 He who knows that this body is like froth, and has learnt that it is as unsubstantial as a mirage, will break the flower-pointed arrow of Mâra, and never see the king of death.

47 Death carries off a man who is gathering flowers, and whose mind is distracted, as a flood carries off a sleeping village.

48 Death subdues a man who is gathering flowers, and whose mind is distracted, before he is satiated in his pleasures.

49 As the bee collects nectar and departs without injuring the flower, or its colour or scent, so let a sage dwell in his village.

50 Not the perversities of others, not their sins of commission or omission, but his own misdeeds and negligences should a sage take notice of.

51 Like a beautiful flower, full of colour, but without scent, are the fine but fruitless words of him who does not act accordingly.

52 But, like a beautiful flower, full of colour and full of scent, are the fine and fruitful words of him who acts accordingly.

53 As many kinds of wreaths can be made from a heap of flowers, so many good things may be achieved by a mortal when once he is born.

54 The scent of flowers does not travel against the wind, nor (that of) sandal-wood, or (of) Tagara and Mallikâ flowers; but the odour of good

people travels even against the wind; a good man pervades every place.

55 Sandal-wood or Tagara, a lotus-flower, or a Vassikî, among these sorts of perfumes, the perfume of virtue is unsurpassed.

56 Mean is the scent that comes from Tagara and sandal-wood;—the perfume of those who possess virtue rises up to the gods as the highest.

57 Of the people who possess these virtues, who live without thoughtlessness, and who are emancipated through true knowledge, Mâra, the tempter, never finds the way.

58, 59 As on a heap of rubbish cast upon the highway the lily will grow full of sweet perfume and delight, thus among those who are mere rubbish the disciple of the truly enlightened Buddha shines forth by his knowledge above the blinded worldling.

CHAPTER V

THE FOOL

60 Long is the night to him who is awake; long
is a mile to him who is tired; long is life to the
foolish who do not know the true law.

61 If a traveller does not meet with one who is
his better, or his equal, let him firmly keep to
his solitary journey; there is no companionship
with a fool.

62 'These sons belong to me, and this wealth
belongs to me,' with such thoughts a fool is
tormented. He himself does not belong to
himself; how much less sons and wealth?

63 The fool who knows his foolishness, is wise at
least so far. But a fool who thinks himself wise,
he is called a fool indeed.

64 If a fool be associated with a wise man even all

his life, he will perceive the truth as little as a spoon perceives the taste of soup.

65 If an intelligent man be associated for one minute only with a wise man, he will soon perceive the truth, as the tongue perceives the taste of soup.

66 Fools of poor understanding have themselves for their greatest enemies, for they do evil deeds which bear bitter fruits.

67 That deed is not well done of which a man must repent, and the reward of which he receives crying and with a tearful face.

68 No, that deed is well done of which a man does not repent, and the reward of which he receives gladly and cheerfully.

69 As long as the evil deed done does not bear fruit, the fool thinks it is like honey; but when it ripens, then the fool suffers grief.

70 Let a fool month after month eat his food (like an ascetic) with the tip of a blade of Kusa grass, yet is he not worth the sixteenth particle of those who have well weighed the law.

71 An evil deed, like newly-drawn milk, does not turn (suddenly); smouldering, like fire covered by ashes, it follows the fool.

72 And when the evil deed, after it has become known, turns to sorrow for the fool, then it destroys his bright lot, nay, it cleaves his head.

73 Let the fool wish for a false reputation, for precedence among the Bhikshus, for lordship in the convents, for worship among other people!

74 'May both the layman and he who has left the world think that this is done by me; may they be subject to me in everything which is to be done or is not to be done,' thus is the mind of the fool, and his desire and pride increase.

75 'One is the road that leads to wealth, another the road that leads to Nirvâna;' if the Bhikshu, the disciple of Buddha, has learnt this, he will not yearn for honour, he will strive after separation from the world.

CHAPTER VI

THE WISE MAN (PANDITA)

76 If you see a man who shows you what is to be avoided, who administers reproofs, and is intelligent, follow that wise man as you would one who tells of hidden treasures; it will be better, not worse, for him who follows him.

77 Let him admonish, let him teach, let him forbid what is improper!—he will be beloved of the good, by the bad he will be hated.

78 Do not have evil-doers for friends, do not have low people for friends: have virtuous people for friends, have for friends the best of men.

79 He who drinks in the law lives happily with a serene mind: the sage rejoices always in the law, as preached by the elect (Ariyas).

80 Well-makers lead the water (wherever they like); fletchers bend the arrow; carpenters bend a log of wood; wise people fashion themselves.

81 As a solid rock is not shaken by the wind, wise people falter not amidst blame and praise.

82 Wise people, after they have listened to the laws, become serene, like a deep, smooth, and still lake.

83 Good men indeed walk (warily) under all circumstances; good men speak not out of a desire for sensual gratification; whether touched by happiness or sorrow wise people never appear elated or depressed.

84 If, whether for his own sake, or for the sake of others, a man wishes neither for a son, nor for wealth, nor for lordship, and if he does not wish for his own success by unfair means, then he is good, wise, and virtuous.

85 Few are there among men who arrive at the other shore (become Arhats); the other people here run up and down the shore.

86 But those who, when the law has been well preached to them, follow the law, will pass over the dominion of death, however difficult to cross.

87, 88 A wise man should leave the dark state (of ordinary life), and follow the bright state (of the Bhikshu). After going from his home to a homeless state, he should in his retirement look for enjoyment where enjoyment seemed difficult. Leaving all pleasures behind, and calling nothing his own, the wise man should purge himself from all the troubles of the mind.

89 Those whose mind is well grounded in the (seven) elements of knowledge, who without clinging to anything, rejoice in freedom from attachment, whose appetites have been conquered, and who are full of light, they are free (even) in this world.

CHAPTER VII

TIIE VENERABLE (ARHAT)

90 There is no suffering for him who has finished his journey, and abandoned grief, who has freed himself on all sides, and thrown off all fetters.

91 They exert themselves with their thoughts well-collected, they do not tarry in their abode; like swans who have left their lake, they leave their house and home.

92 Men who have no riches, who live on recognised food, who have perceived void and unconditioned freedom (Nirvâna), their path is difficult to understand, like that of birds in the air.

93 He whose appetites are stilled, who is not absorbed in enjoyment, who has perceived void and unconditioned freedom (Nirvâna), his path is difficult to understand, like that of birds in the air.

94 The gods even envy him whose senses, like horses well broken in by the driver, have been subdued, who is free from pride, and free from appetites;

95 Such a one who does his duty is tolerant like the earth, or like a threshold; he is like a lake without mud; no new births are in store for him.

96 His thought is quiet, quiet are his word and deed, when he has obtained freedom by true knowledge, when he has thus become a quiet man.

97 The man who is free from credulity, but knows the uncreated, who has cut all ties, removed all temptations, renounced all desires, he is the greatest of men.

98 In a hamlet or in a forest, on sea or on dry land, wherever venerable persons (Arahanta) dwell, that place is delightful.

99 Forests are delightful; where the world finds no delight, there the passionless will find delight, for they look not for pleasures.

CHAPTER VIII

THE THOUSANDS

100 Even though a speech be a thousand (of words), but made up of senseless words, one word of sense is better, which if a man hears, he becomes quiet.

101 Even though a Gâthâ (poem) be a thousand (of words), but made up of senseless words, one word of a Gâthâ is better, which if a man hears, he becomes quiet.

102 Though a man recite a hundred Gâthâs made up of senseless words, one word of the law is better, which if a man hears, he becomes quiet.

103 If one man conquer in battle a thousand times thousand men, and if another conquer himself, he is the greatest of conquerors.

104, 105 One's own self conquered is better than all other people; not even a god, a Gandharva, not Mâra with Brahman could change into defeat the victory of a man who has vanquished himself, and always lives under restraint.

106 If a man for a hundred years sacrifice month by month with a thousand, and if he but for one moment pay homage to a man whose soul is grounded (in true knowledge), better is that homage than a sacrifice for a hundred years.

107 If a man for a hundred years worship Agni (fire) in the forest, and if he but for one moment pay homage to a man whose soul is grounded (in true knowledge), better is that homage than sacrifice for a hundred years.

108 Whatever a man sacrifice in this world as an offering or as an oblation for a whole year in order to gain merit, the whole of it is not worth a quarter (a farthing); reverence shown to the righteous is better.

109 He who always greets and constantly reveres the aged, four things will increase to him, viz. life, beauty, happiness, power.

110 But he who lives a hundred years, vicious and unrestrained, a life of one day is better if a man is virtuous and reflecting.

111 And he who lives a hundred years, ignorant and unrestrained, a life of one day is better if a man is wise and reflecting.

112 And he who lives a hundred years, idle and weak, a life of one day is better if a man has attained firm strength.

113 And he who lives a hundred years, not seeing beginning and end, a life of one day is better if a man sees beginning and end.

114 And he who lives a hundred years, not seeing the immortal place, a life of one day is better if a man sees the immortal place.

115 And he who lives a hundred years, not seeing the highest law, a life of one day is better if a man sees the highest law.

CHAPTER IX

EVIL

116 A man should hasten towards the good, and should keep his thought away from evil; if a man does what is good slothfully, his mind delights in evil.

117 If a man commits a sin, let him not do it again; let him not delight in sin: the accumulation of evil is painful.

118 If a man does what is good, let him do it again; let him delight in it: the accumulation of good is delightful.

119 Even an evil-doer sees happiness so long as his evil deed does not ripen; but when his evil deed ripens, then does the evil-doer see evil.

120 Even a good man sees evil days so long as his good deed does not ripen; but when his good deed ripens, then does the good man see good things.

121 Let no man think lightly of evil, saying in his heart, It will not come nigh unto me. Even by the falling of water-drops a water-pot is filled; the fool becomes full of evil, even if he gather it little by little.

122 Let no man think lightly of good, saying in his heart, It will not come nigh unto me. Even by the falling of water-drops a water-pot is filled; the wise man becomes full of good, even if he gather it little by little.

123 Let a man avoid evil deeds, as a merchant, if he has few companions and carries much wealth, avoids a dangerous road; as a man who loves life avoids poison.

124 He who has no wound on his hand, may touch poison with his hand; poison does not affect one who has no wound; nor is there evil for one who does not commit evil.

125 If a man offend a harmless, pure, and innocent person, the evil falls back upon that fool, like light dust thrown up against the wind.

126 Some people are born again; evil-doers go to hell; righteous people go to heaven; those who are free from all worldly desires attain Nirvâna.

127 Not in the sky, not in the midst of the sea, not if we enter into the clefts of the mountains, is there known a spot in the whole world where a man might be freed from an evil deed.

128 Not in the sky, not in the midst of the sea, not if we enter into the clefts of the mountains, is there known a spot in the whole world where death could not overcome (the mortal).

CHAPTER X

PUNISHMENT

129 All men tremble at punishment, all men fear
death; remember that you are like unto them,
and do not kill, nor cause slaughter.

130 All men tremble at punishment, all men love
life; remember that thou art like unto them, and
do not kill, nor cause slaughter.

131 He who, seeking his own happiness, punishes
or kills beings who also long for happiness, will
not find happiness after death.

132 He who seeking his own happiness does
not punish or kill beings who also long for
happiness, will find happiness after death.

133 Do not speak harshly to anybody; those who
are spoken to will answer thee in the same way.
Angry speech is painful, blows for blows will
touch thee.

134 If, like a shattered metal plate (gong), thou utter nothing, then thou hast reached Nirvâna; anger is not known to thee.

135 As a cowherd with his staff drives his cows into the stable, so do Age and Death drive the life of men.

136 A fool does not know when he commits his evil deeds: but the wicked man burns by his own deeds, as if burnt by fire.

137 He who inflicts pain on innocent and harmless persons, will soon come to one of these ten states:

138 He will have cruel suffering, loss, injury of the body, heavy affliction, or loss of mind,

139 Or a misfortune coming from the king, or a fearful accusation, or loss of relations, or destruction of treasures,

140 Or lightning-fire will burn his houses; and when his body is destroyed, the fool will go to hell.

141 Not nakedness, not platted hair, not dirt, not fasting, or lying on the earth, not rubbing with dust, not sitting motionless, can purify a mortal who has not overcome desires.

142 He who, though dressed in fine apparel, exercises tranquillity, is quiet, subdued, restrained, chaste, and has ceased to find fault with all other beings, he indeed is a Brâhmana, an ascetic (sramana), a friar (bhikshu).

143 Is there in this world any man so restrained by shame that he does not provoke reproof, as a noble horse the whip?

144 Like a noble horse when touched by the whip, be ye strenuous and eager, and by faith, by virtue, by energy, by meditation, by discernment of the law you will overcome this great pain, perfect in knowledge and in behaviour, and never forgetful.

145 Well-makers lead the water (wherever they like); fletchers bend the arrow; carpenters bend a log of wood; good people fashion themselves.

CHAPTER XI

OLD AGE

146 How is there laughter, how is there joy, as this world is always burning? Do you not seek a light, ye who are surrounded by darkness?

147 Look at this dressed-up lump, covered with wounds, joined together, sickly, full of many schemes, but which has no strength, no hold!

148 This body is wasted, full of sickness, and frail; this heap of corruption breaks to pieces, life indeed ends in death.

149 After one has looked at those grey bones, thrown away like gourds in the autumn, what pleasure is there (left in life)!

150 After a stronghold has been made of the bones, it is covered with flesh and blood, and there dwell in it old age and death, pride and deceit.

151 The brilliant chariots of kings are destroyed, the body also approaches destruction, but the virtue of good people never approaches destruction,—thus do the good say to the good.

152 A man who has learnt little, grows old like an ox; his flesh grows, but his knowledge does not grow.

153, 154 Looking for the maker of this tabernacle, I have run through a course of many births, not finding him; and painful is birth again and again. But now, maker of the tabernacle, thou hast been seen; thou shalt not make up this tabernacle again. All thy rafters are broken, thy ridge-pole is sundered; the mind, approaching the Eternal (visankhâra, nirvâna), has attained to the extinction of all desires.

155 Men who have not observed proper discipline, and have not gained wealth in their youth, perish like old herons in a lake without fish.

156 Men who have not observed proper discipline, and have not gained wealth in their youth, lie, like broken bows, sighing after the past.

CHAPTER XII

SELF

157 If a man hold himself dear, let him watch himself carefully; during one at least out of the three watches a wise man should be watchful.

158 Let each man direct himself first to what is proper, then let him teach others; thus a wise man will not suffer.

159 If a man make himself as he teaches others to be, then, being himself well subdued, he may subdue (others); for one's own self is difficult to subdue.

160 Self is the lord of self, who else could be the lord? With self well subdued, a man finds a lord such as few can find.

161 The evil done by oneself, self-begotten, selfbred, crushes the foolish, as a diamond breaks even a precious stone.

162 He whose wickedness is very great brings himself down to that state where his enemy wishes him to be, as a creeper does with the tree which it surrounds.

163 Bad deeds, and deeds hurtful to ourselves, are easy to do; what is beneficial and good, that is very difficult to do.

164 The foolish man who scorns the rule of the venerable (Arahat), of the elect (Ariya), of the virtuous, and follows a false doctrine, he bears fruit to his own destruction, like the fruits of the Katthaka reed.

165 By oneself the evil is done, by oneself one suffers; by oneself evil is left undone, by oneself one is purified. The pure and the impure (stand and fall) by themselves, no one can purify another.

166 Let no one forget his own duty for the sake of another's, however great; let a man, after he has discerned his own duty, be always attentive to his duty.

CHAPTER XIII

THE WORLD

167 Do not follow the evil law! Do not live on in thoughtlessness! Do not follow false doctrine! Be not a friend of the world.

168 Rouse thyself! do not be idle! Follow the law of virtue! The virtuous rests in bliss in this world and in the next.

169 Follow the law of virtue; do not follow that of sin. The virtuous rests in bliss in this world and in the next.

170 Look upon the world as you would on a bubble, look upon it as you would on a mirage: the king of death does not see him who thus looks down upon the world.

171 Come, look at this world, glittering like a royal chariot; the foolish are immersed in it, but the wise do not touch it.

172 He who formerly was reckless and afterwards became sober, brightens up this world, like the moon when freed from clouds.

173 He whose evil deeds are covered by good deeds, brightens up this world, like the moon when freed from clouds.

174 This world is dark, few only can see here; a few only go to heaven, like birds escaped from the net.

175 The swans go on the path of the sun, they go miraculously through the ether; the wise are led out of this world, when they have conquered Mâra and his train.

176 If a man has transgressed the one law, and speaks lies, and scoffs at another world, there is no evil he will not do.

177 The uncharitable do not go to the world of the gods; fools only do not praise liberality; a

wise man rejoices in liberality, and through it becomes blessed in the other world.

178 Better than sovereignty over the earth, better than going to heaven, better than lordship over all worlds, is the reward of Sotâpatti, the first step in holiness.

CHAPTER XIV

THE BUDDHA (THE AWAKENED)

179 He whose conquest cannot be conquered again, into whose conquest no one in this world enters, by what track can you lead him, the Awakened, the Omniscient, the trackless?

180 He whom no desire with its snares and poisons can lead astray, by what track can you lead him, the Awakened, the Omniscient, the trackless?

181 Even the gods envy those who are awakened and not forgetful, who are given to meditation, who are wise, and who delight in the repose of retirement (from the world).

182 Difficult (to obtain) is the conception of men, difficult is the life of mortals, difficult is the hearing of the True Law, difficult is the birth of the Awakened (the attainment of Buddhahood).

183 Not to commit any sin, to do good, and to purify one's mind, that is the teaching of (all) the Awakened.

184 The Awakened call patience the highest penance, long-suffering the highest Nirvâna; for he is not an anchorite (pravragita) who strikes others, he is not an ascetic (sramana) who insults others.

185 Not to blame, not to strike, to live restrained under the law, to be moderate in eating, to sleep and sit alone, and to dwell on the highest thoughts,—this is the teaching of the Awakened.

186 There is no satisfying lusts, even by a shower of gold pieces; he who knows that lusts have a short taste and cause pain, he is wise;

187 Even in heavenly pleasures he finds no satisfaction, the disciple who is fully awakened delights only in the destruction of all desires.

188 Men, driven by fear, go to many a refuge, to mountains and forests, to groves and sacred trees.

189 But that is not a safe refuge, that is not the best refuge; a man is not delivered from all pains after having gone to that refuge.

190 He who takes refuge with Buddha, the Law, and the Church; he who, with clear understanding, sees the four holy truths:—

191 Viz. pain, the origin of pain, the destruction of pain, and the eightfold holy way that leads to the quieting of pain;—

192 That is the safe refuge, that is the best refuge; having gone to that refuge, a man is delivered from all pain.

193 A supernatural person (a Buddha) is not easily found, he is not born everywhere. Wherever such a sage is born, that race prospers.

194 Happy is the arising of the awakened, happy is the teaching of the True Law, happy is peace in the church, happy is the devotion of those who are at peace.

195, 196 He who pays homage to those who deserve homage, whether the awakened (Buddha) or their disciples, those who have overcome the host (of evils), and crossed the flood of sorrow, he who pays homage to such as have found deliverance and know no fear, his merit can never be measured by anybody.

CHAPTER XV

HAPPINESS

197 We live happily indeed, not hating those who hate us! among men who hate us we dwell free from hatred!

198 We live happily indeed, free from ailments among the ailing! among men who are ailing let us dwell free from ailments!

199 We live happily indeed, free from greed among the greedy! among men who are greedy let us dwell free from greed!

200 We live happily indeed, though we call nothing our own! We shall be like the bright gods, feeding on happiness!

201 Victory breeds hatred, for the conquered is unhappy. He who has given up both victory and defeat, he, the contented, is happy.

202 There is no fire like passion; there is no losing throw like hatred; there is no pain like this body; there is no happiness higher than rest.

203 Hunger is the worst of diseases, the elements of the body the greatest evil; if one knows this truly, that is Nirvâna, the highest happiness.

204 Health is the greatest of gifts, contentedness the best riches; trust is the best of relationships, Nirvâna the highest happiness.

205 He who has tasted the sweetness of solitude and tranquillity, is free from fear and free from sin, while he tastes the sweetness of drinking in the law.

206 The sight of the elect (Arya) is good, to live with them is always happiness; if a man does not see fools, he will be truly happy.

207 He who walks in the company of fools suffers a long way; company with fools, as with an enemy, is always painful; company with the wise is pleasure, like meeting with kinsfolk.

208 Therefore, one ought to follow the wise, the intelligent, the learned, the much enduring, the

dutiful, the elect; one ought to follow such a good and wise man, as the moon follows the path of the stars.

CHAPTER XVI

PLEASURE

209 He who gives himself to vanity, and does not give himself to meditation, forgetting the real aim (of life) and grasping at pleasure, will in time envy him who has exerted himself in meditation.

210 Let no man ever cling to what is pleasant, or to what is unpleasant. Not to see what is pleasant is pain, and it is pain to see what is unpleasant.

211 Let, therefore, no man love anything; loss of the beloved is evil. Those who love nothing, and hate nothing, have no fetters.

212 From pleasure comes grief, from pleasure comes fear; he who is free from pleasure knows neither grief nor fear.

213 From affection comes grief, from affection comes fear; he who is free from affection knows neither grief nor fear

214 From lust comes grief, from lust comes fear; he who is free from lust knows neither grief nor fear.

215 From love comes grief, from love comes fear; he who is free from love knows neither grief nor fear.

216 From greed comes grief, from greed comes fear; he who is free from greed knows neither grief nor fear.

217 He who possesses virtue and intelligence, who is just, speaks the truth, and does what is his own business, him the world will hold dear.

218 He in whom a desire for the Ineffable (Nirvâna) has sprung up, who in his mind is satisfied, and whose thoughts are not bewildered by love, he is called ûrdhvamsrotas (carried upwards by the stream).

219 Kinsmen, friends, and lovers salute a man who has been long away, and returns safe from afar.

220 In like manner his good works receive him who has done good, and has gone from this world to the other;—as kinsmen receive a friend on his return.

CHAPTER XVII

ANGER

221 Let a man leave anger, let him forsake pride, let him overcome all bondage! No sufferings befall the man who is not attached to name and form, and who calls nothing his own.

222 He who holds back rising anger like a rolling chariot, him I call a real driver; other people are but holding the reins.

223 Let a man overcome anger by love, let him overcome evil by good; let him overcome the greedy by liberality, the liar by truth!

224 Speak the truth, do not yield to anger; give, if thou art asked for little; by these three steps thou wilt go near the gods.

225 The sages who injure nobody, and who always control their body, they will go to the

unchangeable place (Nirvâna), where, if they have gone, they will suffer no more.

226 Those who are ever watchful, who study day and night, and who strive after Nirvâna, their passions will come to an end.

227 This is an old saying, O Atula, this is not as if of to-day: 'They blame him who sits silent, they blame him who speaks much, they also blame him who says little; there is no one on earth who is not blamed.'

228 There never was, there never will be, nor is there now, a man who is always blamed, or a man who is always praised.

229, 230 But he whom those who discriminate praise continually day after day, as without blemish, wise, rich in knowledge and virtue, who would dare to blame him, like a coin made of gold from the Gambû river? Even the gods praise him, he is praised even by Brahman.

231 Beware of bodily anger, and control thy body! Leave the sins of the body, and with thy body practise virtue!

232 Beware of the anger of the tongue, and control thy tongue! Leave the sins of the tongue, and practise virtue with thy tongue!

233 Beware of the anger of the mind, and control thy mind! Leave the sins of the mind, and practise virtue with thy mind!

234 The wise who control their body, who control their tongue, the wise who control their mind, are indeed well controlled.

CHAPTER XVIII

IMPURITY

235 Thou art now like a sear leaf, the messengers of death (Yama) have come near to thee; thou standest at the door of thy departure, and thou hast no provision for thy journey.

236 Make thyself an island, work hard, be wise! When thy impurities are blown away, and thou art free from guilt, thou wilt enter into the heavenly world of the elect (Ariya).

237 Thy life has come to an end, thou art come near to death (Yama), there is no resting-place for thee on the road, and thou hast no provision for thy journey.

238 Make thyself an island, work hard, be wise! When thy impurities are blown away, and thou art free from guilt, thou wilt not enter again into birth and decay.

239 Let a wise man blow off the impurities of himself, as a smith blows off the impurities of silver, one by one, little by little, and from time to time.

240 As the impurity which springs from the iron, when it springs from it, destroys it; thus do a transgressor's own works lead him to the evil path.

241 The taint of prayers is non-repetition; the taint of houses, non-repair; the taint of complexion is sloth; the taint of a watchman, thoughtlessness.

242 Bad conduct is the taint of woman, niggardliness the taint of a benefactor; tainted are all evil ways, in this world and in the next.

243 But there is a taint worse than all taints,— ignorance is the greatest taint. O mendicants! throw off that taint, and become taintless!

244 Life is easy to live for a man who is without shame, a crow hero, a mischief-maker, an insulting, bold, and wretched fellow.

245 But life is hard to live for a modest man, who always looks for what is pure, who is disinterested, quiet, spotless, and intelligent.

246 He who destroys life, who speaks untruth, who in the world takes what is not given him, who goes to another man's wife;

247 And the man who gives himself to drinking intoxicating liquors, he, even in this world, digs up his own root.

248 O man, know this, that the unrestrained are in a bad state; take care that greediness and vice do not bring thee to grief for a long time!

249 The world gives according to their faith or according to their pleasure: if a man frets about the food and the drink given to others, he will find no rest either by day or by night.

250 He in whom that feeling is destroyed, and taken out with the very root, finds rest by day and by night.

251 There is no fire like passion, there is no shark like hatred, there is no snare like folly, there is no torrent like greed.

252 The fault of others is easily perceived, but that of oneself is difficult to perceive: a man winnows his neighbour's faults like chaff, but his own fault he hides, as a cheat hides the bad die from the player.

253 If a man looks after the faults of others, and is always inclined to be offended, his own passions will grow, and he is far from the destruction of passions.

254 There is no path through the air, a man is not a Samana outwardly. The world delights in vanity, the Tathâgatas (the Buddhas) are free from vanity.

255 There is no path through the air, a man is not a Samana outwardly. No creatures are eternal; but the awakened (Buddha) are never shaken.

CHAPTER XIX

THE JUST

256, 257 A man is not just if he carries a matter by
violence; no, he who distinguishes both right
and wrong, who is learned and guides others,
not by violence, but by the same law, being a
guardian of the law and intelligent, he is called
just.

258 A man is not learned because he talks much; he
who is patient, free from hatred and fear, he is
called learned.

259 A man is not a supporter of the law because he
talks much; even if a man has learnt little, but
sees the law bodily, he is a supporter of the law,
a man who never neglects the law.

260 A man is not an elder because his head is grey;
his age may be ripe, but he is called 'Old-in-
vain.'

261 He in whom there is truth, virtue, pity, restraint, moderation, he who is free from impurity and is wise, he is called an elder.

262 An envious, stingy, dishonest man does not become respectable by means of much talking only, or by the beauty of his complexion.

263 He in whom all this is destroyed, and taken out with the very root, he, when freed from hatred and wise, is called respectable.

264 Not by tonsure does an undisciplined man who speaks falsehood become a Samana; can a man be a Samana who is still held captive by desire and greediness?

265 He who always quiets the evil, whether small or large, he is called a Samana (a quiet man), because he has quieted all evil.

266 A man is not a mendicant (Bhikshu) simply because he asks others for alms; he who adopts the whole law is a Bhikshu, not he who only begs.

267 He who is above good and evil, who is chaste, who with care passes through the world, he indeed is called a Bhikshu.

268, 269 A man is not a Muni because he observes silence (mona, i. e. mauna), if he is foolish and ignorant; but the wise who, as with the balance, chooses the good and avoids evil, he is a Muni, and is a Muni thereby; he who in this world weighs both sides is called a Muni.

270 A man is not an elect (Ariya) because he injuries living creatures; because he has pity on all living creatures, therefore is a man called Ariya.

271, 272 Not only by discipline and vows, not only by much learning, not by entering into a trance, not by sleeping alone, do I earn the happiness of release which no worldling can know. O Bhikshu, he who has obtained the extinction of desires, has obtained confidence.

CHAPTER XX

THE WAY

273 The best of ways is the eightfold; the best of truths the four words; the best of virtues passionlessness; the best of men he who has eyes to see.

274 This is the way, there is no other that leads to the purifying of intelligence. Go on this path! This is the confusion of Mâra (the tempter).

275 If you go on this way, you will make an end of pain! The way was preached by me, when I had understood the removal of the thorns (in the flesh).

276 You yourself must make an effort. The Tathâgatas (Buddhas) are only preachers. The thoughtful who enter the way are freed from the bondage of Mâra.

277 'All created things perish,' he who knows and sees this becomes passive in pain; this is the way to purity.

278 'All created things are grief and pain,' he who knows and sees this becomes passive in pain: this is the way that leads to purity.

279 'All forms are unreal,' he who knows and sees this becomes passive in pain; this is the way that leads to purity.

280 He who does not rouse himself when it is time to rise, who, though young and strong, is full of sloth, whose will and thought are weak, that lazy and idle man never finds the way to knowledge.

281 Watching his speech, well restrained in mind, let a man never commit any wrong with his body! Let a man but keep these three roads of action clear, and he will achieve the way which is taught by the wise.

282 Through zeal knowledge is gotten, through lack of zeal knowledge is lost; let a man who knows this double path of gain and loss thus place himself that knowledge may grow.

283 Cut down the whole forest (of desires), not a
tree only! Danger comes out of the forest (of
desires). When you have cut down both the
forest (of desires) and its undergrowth, then,
Bhikshus, you will be rid of the forest and of
desires!

284 So long as the desire of man towards women,
even the smallest, is not destroyed, so long is
his mind in bondage, as the calf that drinks
milk is to its mother.

285 Cut out the love of self, like an autumn lotus,
with thy hand! Cherish the road of peace.
Nirvâna has been shown by Sugata (Buddha).

286 'Here I shall dwell in the rain, here in winter
and summer,' thus the fool meditates, and does
not think of death.

287 Death comes and carries off that man, honoured
for his children and flocks, his mind distracted,
as a flood carries off a sleeping village.

288 Sons are no help, nor a father, nor relations;
there is no help from kinsfolk for one whom
death has seized.

289 A wise and well-behaved man who knows the meaning of this, should quickly clear the way that leads to Nirvâna.

CHAPTER XXI

MISCELLANEOUS

290 If by leaving a small pleasure one sees a great pleasure, let a wise man leave the small pleasure, and look to the great.

291 He who, by causing pain to others, wishes to obtain pleasure for himself, he, entangled in the bonds of hatred, will never be free from hatred.

292 What ought to be done is neglected, what ought not to be done is done; the desires of unruly, thoughtless people are always increasing.

293 But they whose whole watchfulness is always directed to their body, who do not follow what ought not to be done, and who steadfastly do what ought to be done, the desires of such watchful and wise people will come to an end.

294 A true Brâhmaṇa goes scatheless, though he have killed father and mother, and two valiant kings, though he has destroyed a kingdom with all its subjects.

295 A true Brâhmaṇa goes scatheless, though he have killed father and mother, and two holy kings, and an eminent man besides.

296 The disciples of Gotama (Buddha) are always well awake, and their thoughts day and night are always set on Buddha.

297 The disciples of Gotama are always well awake, and their thoughts day and night are always set on the law.

298 The disciples of Gotama are always well awake, and their thoughts day and night are always set on the church.

299 The disciples of Gotama are always well awake, and their thoughts day and night are always set on their body.

300 The disciples of Gotama are always well awake, and their mind day and night always delights in compassion.

301 The disciples of Gotama are always well awake, and their mind day and night always delights in meditation.

302 It is hard to leave the world (to become a friar), it is hard to enjoy the world; hard is the monastery, painful are the houses; painful it is to dwell with equals (to share everything in common), and the itinerant mendicant is beset with pain. Therefore let no man be an itinerant mendicant, and he will not be beset with pain.

303 A man full of faith, if endowed with virtue and glory, is respected, whatever place he may choose.

304 Good people shine from afar, like the snowy mountains; bad people are not seen, like arrows shot by night.

305 Sitting alone, lying down alone, walking alone without ceasing, and alone subduing himself, let a man be happy near the edge of a forest.

CHAPTER XXII

THE DOWNWARD COURSE

306 He who says what is not, goes to hell; he also who, having done a thing, says I have not done it. After death both are equal, they are men with evil deeds in the next world.

307 Many men whose shoulders are covered with the yellow gown are ill-conditioned and unrestrained; such evil-doers by their evil deeds go to hell.

308 Better it would be to swallow a heated iron ball, like flaring fire, than that a bad unrestrained fellow should live on the charity of the land.

309 Four things does a reckless man gain who covets his neighbour's wife,—demerit, an uncomfortable bed, thirdly punishment, and lastly, hell.

310 There is demerit, and the evil way (to hell), there is the short pleasure of the frightened in the arms of the frightened, and the king imposes heavy punishment; therefore let no man think of his neighbour's wife.

311 As a grass-blade, if badly grasped, cuts the arm, badly-practised asceticism leads to hell.

312 An act carelessly performed, a broken vow, and hesitating obedience to discipline (Brahma-kariyam), all this brings no great reward.

313 If anything is to be done, let a man do it, let him attack it vigorously! A careless pilgrim only scatters the dust of his passions more widely.

314 An evil deed is better left undone, for a man repents of it afterwards; a good deed is better done, for having done it, one does not repent.

315 Like a well-guarded frontier fort, with defences within and without, so let a man guard himself. Not a moment should escape, for they who allow the right moment to pass, suffer pain when they are in hell.

316 They who are ashamed of what they ought not to be ashamed of, and are not ashamed of what they ought to be ashamed of, such men, embracing false doctrines, enter the evil path.

317 They who fear when they ought not to fear, and fear not when they ought to fear, such men, embracing false doctrines, enter the evil path.

318 They who see sin where there is no sin, and see no sin where there is sin, such men, embracing false doctrines, enter the evil path.

319 They who see sin where there is sin, and no sin where there is no sin, such men, embracing the true doctrine, enter the good path.

CHAPTER XXIII

THE ELEPHANT

320 Silently I endured abuse as the elephant in battle endures the arrow sent from the bow: for the world is ill-natured.

321 They lead a tamed elephant to battle, the king mounts a tamed elephant; the tamed is the best among men, he who silently endures abuse.

322 Mules are good, if tamed, and noble Sindhu horses, and elephants with large tusks; but he who tames himself is better still.

323 For with these animals does no man reach the untrodden country (Nirvâna), where a tamed man goes on a tamed animal, viz. on his own well-tamed self.

324 The elephant called Dhanapâlaka, his temples running with pungent sap, and who is difficult

to hold, does not eat a morsel when bound; the elephant longs for the elephant grove.

325 If a man becomes fat and a great eater, if he is sleepy and rolls himself about, that fool, like a hog fed on grains, is born again and again.

326 This mind of mine went formerly wandering about as it liked, as it listed, as it pleased; but I shall now hold it in thoroughly, as the rider who holds the hook holds in the furious elephant.

327 Be not thoughtless, watch your thoughts! Draw yourself out of the evil way, like an elephant sunk in mud.

328 If a man find a prudent companion who walks with him, is wise, and lives soberly, he may walk with him, overcoming all dangers, happy, but considerate.

329 If a man find no prudent companion who walks with him, is wise, and lives soberly, let him walk alone, like a king who has left his conquered country behind,—like an elephant in the forest.

330 It is better to live alone, there is no companionship with a fool; let a man walk alone, let him commit no sin, with few wishes, like an elephant in the forest.

331 If the occasion arises, friends are pleasant; enjoyment is pleasant, whatever be the cause; a good work is pleasant in the hour of death; the giving up of all grief is pleasant.

332 Pleasant in the world is the state of a mother, pleasant the state of a father, pleasant the state of a Samana, pleasant the state of a Brâhmana.

333 Pleasant is virtue lasting to old age, pleasant is a faith firmly rooted; pleasant is attainment of intelligence, pleasant is avoiding of sins.

CHAPTER XXIV

THIRST

334 The thirst of a thoughtless man grows like a creeper; he runs from life to life, like a monkey seeking fruit in the forest.

335 Whomsoever this fierce poisonous thirst overcomes, in this world, his sufferings increase like the abounding Bîrana grass.

336 But from him who overcomes this fierce thirst, difficult to be conquered in this world, sufferings fall off, like water-drops from a lotus leaf.

337 This salutary word I tell you, 'Do ye, as many as are here assembled, dig up the root of thirst, as he who wants the sweet-scented Usîra root must dig up the Bîrana grass, that Mâra (the tempter) may not crush you again and again, as the stream crushes the reeds.'

338 As a tree, even though it has been cut down, is firm so long as its root is safe, and grows again, thus, unless the feeders of thirst are destroyed, this pain (of life) will return again and again.

339 He whose thirty-six streams are strongly flowing in the channels of pleasure, the waves will carry away that misguided man, viz. his desires which are set on passion.

340 The channels run everywhere, the creeper (of passion) stands sprouting; if you see the creeper springing up, cut its root by means of knowledge.

341 A creature's pleasures are extravagant and luxurious; given up to pleasure and deriving happiness, men undergo (again and again) birth and decay.

342 Beset with lust, men run about like a snared hare; held in fetters and bonds, they undergo pain for a long time, again and again.

343 Beset with lust, men run about like a snared hare; let therefore the mendicant drive out thirst, by striving after passionlessness for himself.

344 He who having got rid of the forest (of lust) (i.e. after having reached Nirvâna) gives himself over to forest-life (i.e. to lust), and who, when free from the forest (i.e. from lust), runs to the forest (i.e. to lust), look at that man! though free, he runs into bondage.

345 Wise people do not call that a strong fetter which is made of iron, wood, or hemp; passionately strong is the care for precious stones and rings, for sons and a wife.

346 That fetter wise people call strong which drags down, yields, but is difficult to undo; after having cut this at last, people leave the world, free from cares, and leaving the pleasures of love behind.

347 Those who are slaves to passions, run down the stream (of desires), as a spider runs down the web which he has made himself; when they have cut this, at last, wise people go onwards, free from cares, leaving all pain behind.

348 Give up what is before, give up what is behind, give up what is between, when thou goest to the other shore of existence; if thy mind is

altogether free, thou wilt not again enter into birth and decay.

349 If a man is tossed about by doubts, full of strong passions, and yearning only for what is delightful, his thirst will grow more and more, and he will indeed make his fetters strong.

350 If a man delights in quieting doubts, and, always reflecting, dwells on what is not delightful (the impurity of the body, &c.), he certainly will remove, nay, he will cut the fetter of Mâra.

351 He who has reached the consummation, who does not tremble, who is without thirst and without sin, he has broken all the thorns of life: this will be his last body.

352 He who is without thirst and without affection, who understands the words and their interpretation, who knows the order of letters (those which are before and which are after), he has received his last body, he is called the great sage, the great man.

353 'I have conquered all, I know all, in all conditions of life I am free from taint; I have left all, and through the destruction of thirst I am free; having learnt myself, whom should I indicate (as my teacher)?'

354 The gift of the law exceeds all gifts; the sweetness of the law exceeds all sweetness; the delight in the law exceeds all delights; the extinction of thirst overcomes all pain.

355 Riches destroy the foolish, if they look not for the other shore; the foolish by his thirst for riches destroys himself, as if he were (destroying) others.

356 The fields are damaged by weeds, mankind is damaged by passion: therefore a gift bestowed on the passionless brings great reward.

357 The fields are damaged by weeds, mankind is damaged by hatred: therefore a gift bestowed on those who do not hate brings great reward.

358 The fields are damaged by weeds, mankind is damaged by vanity: therefore a gift bestowed

on those who are free from vanity brings great reward.

359 The fields are damaged by weeds, mankind is damaged by lust: therefore a gift bestowed on those who are free from lust brings great reward.

CHAPTER XXV

THE BHIKSHU (MENDICANT)

360 Restraint in the eye is good, good is restraint in the ear, in the nose restraint is good, good is restraint in the tongue.

361 In the body restraint is good, good is restraint in speech, in thought restraint is good, good is restraint in all things. A Bhikshu, restrained in all things, is freed from all pain.

362 He who controls his hand, he who controls his feet, he who controls his speech, he who is well controlled, he who delights inwardly, who is collected, who is solitary and content, him they call Bhikshu.

363 The Bhikshu who controls his mouth, who speaks wisely and calmly, who teaches the meaning and the law, his word is sweet.

364 He who dwells in the law, delights in the law, meditates on the law, recollects the law, that Bhikshu will never fall away from the true law.

365 Let him not despise what he has received, nor ever envy others: a mendicant who envies others does not obtain peace of mind.

366 A Bhikshu who, though he receives little, does not despise what he has received, even the gods will praise him, if his life is pure, and if he is not slothful.

367 He who never identifies himself with name and form, and does not grieve over what is no more, he indeed is called a Bhikshu.

368 The Bhikshu who behaves with kindness, who is happy in the doctrine of Buddha, will reach the quiet place (Nirvâna), happiness arising from the cessation of natural inclinations.

369 O Bhikshu, empty this boat! if emptied, it will go quickly; having cut off passion and hatred, thou wilt go to Nirvâna.

370 Cut off the five (fetters), leave the five, rise above the five. A Bhikshu, who has escaped from the five fetters, he is called Oghatinna, 'saved from the flood.'

371 Meditate, O Bhikshu, and be not heedless! Do not direct thy thought to what gives pleasure, that thou mayest not for thy heedlessness have to swallow the iron ball (in hell), and that thou mayest not cry out when burning, 'This is pain.'

372 Without knowledge there is no meditation, without meditation there is no knowledge: he who has knowledge and meditation is near unto Nirvâna.

373 A Bhikshu who has entered his empty house, and whose mind is tranquil, feels a more than human delight when he sees the law clearly.

374 As soon as he has considered the origin and destruction of the elements (khandha) of the body, he finds happiness and joy which belong to those who know the immortal (Nirvâna).

375 And this is the beginning here for a wise Bhikshu: watchfulness over the senses, contentedness, restraint under the law; keep noble friends whose life is pure, and who are not slothful.

376 Let him live in charity, let him be perfect in his duties; then in the fulness of delight he will make an end of suffering.

377 As the Vassikâ plant sheds its withered flowers, men should shed passion and hatred, O ye Bhikshus!

378 The Bhikshu whose body and tongue and mind are quieted, who is collected, and has rejected the baits of the world, he is called quiet.

379 Rouse thyself by thyself, examine thyself by thyself, thus self-protected and attentive wilt thou live happily, O Bhikshu!

380 For self is the lord of self, self is the refuge
of self; therefore curb thyself as the merchant
curbs a noble horse.

381 The Bhikshu, full of delight, who is happy in
the doctrine of Buddha will reach the quiet
place (Nirvâna), happiness consisting in the
cessation of natural inclinations.

382 He who, even as a young Bhikshu, applies
himself to the doctrine of Buddha, brightens
up this world, like the moon when free from
clouds.

CHAPTER XXVI

THE BRÂHMANA (ARHAT)

383 Stop the stream valiantly, drive away the desires, O Brâhmana! When you have understood the destruction of all that was made, you will understand that which was not made.

384 If the Brâhmana has reached the other shore in both laws (in restraint and contemplation), all bonds vanish from him who has obtained knowledge.

385 He for whom there is neither the hither nor the further shore, nor both, him, the fearless and unshackled, I call indeed a Brâhmana.

386 He who is thoughtful, blameless, settled, dutiful, without passions, and who has attained the highest end, him I call indeed a Brâhmana.

387 The sun is bright by day, the moon shines by night, the warrior is bright in his armour, the Brâhmana is bright in his meditation; but Buddha, the Awakened, is bright with splendour day and night.

388 Because a man is rid of evil, therefore he is called Brâhmana; because he walks quietly, therefore he is called Samana; because he has sent away his own impurities, therefore he is called Pravragita (Pabbagita, a pilgrim).

389 No one should attack a Brâhmana, but no Brâhmana (if attacked) should let himself fly at his aggressor! Woe to him who strikes a Brâhmana, more woe to him who flies at his aggressor!

390 It advantages a Brâhmana not a little if he holds his mind back from the pleasures of life; the more all wish to injure has vanished, the more all pain will cease.

391 Him I call indeed a Brâhmana who does not offend by body, word, or thought, and is controlled on these three points.

392 He from whom he may learn the law, as taught by the Well-awakened (Buddha), him let him worship assiduously, as the Brâhma*n*a worships the sacrificial fire.

393 A man does not become a Brâhma*n*a by his platted hair, by his family, or by birth; in whom there is truth and righteousness, he is blessed, he is a Brâhma*n*a.

394 What is the use of platted hair, O fool! what of the raiment of goat-skins? Within thee there is ravening, but the outside thou makest clean.

395 The man who wears dirty raiments, who is emaciated and covered with veins, who meditates alone in the forest, him I call indeed a Brâhma*n*a.

396 I do not call a man a Brâhma*n*a because of his origin or of his mother. He is indeed arrogant, and he is wealthy: but the poor, who is free from all attachments, him I call indeed a Brâhma*n*a.

397 Him I call indeed a Brâhma*n*a who after cutting all fetters never trembles, is free from bonds and unshackled.

398 Him I call indeed a Brâhmana who after cutting the strap and the thong, the rope with all that pertains to it, has destroyed all obstacles, and is awakened.

399 Him I call indeed a Brâhmana who, though he has committed no offence, endures reproach, stripes, and bonds, who has endurance for his force, and strength for his army.

400 Him I call indeed a Brâhmana who is free from anger, dutiful, virtuous, without appetites, who is subdued, and has received his last body.

401 Him I call indeed a Brâhmana who does not cling to sensual pleasures, like water on a lotus leaf, like a mustard seed on the point of a needle.

402 Him I call indeed a Brâhmana who, even here, knows the end of his own suffering, has put down his burden, and is unshackled.

403 Him I call indeed a Brâhmana whose knowledge is deep, who possesses wisdom, who knows the right way and the wrong, and has attained the highest end.

404 Him I call indeed a Brâhma*n*a who keeps aloof both from laymen and from mendicants, who frequents no houses, and has but few desires.

405 Him I call indeed a Brâhma*n*a who without hurting any creatures, whether feeble or strong, does not kill nor cause slaughter.

406 Him I call indeed a Brâhma*n*a who is tolerant with the intolerant, mild with the violent, and free from greed among the greedy.

407 Him I call indeed a Brâhma*n*a from whom anger and hatred, pride and hypocrisy have dropt like a mustard seed from the point of a needle.

408 Him I call indeed a Brâhma*n*a who utters true speech, instructive and free from harshness, so that he offend no one.

409 Him I call indeed a Brâhma*n*a who takes nothing in the world that is not given him, be it long or short, small or large, good or bad.

410 Him I call indeed a Brâhma*n*a who fosters no desires for this world or for the next, has no inclinations, and is unshackled.

411 Him I call indeed a Brâhmana who has no interests, and when he has understood (the truth), does not say How, how? and who has reached the depth of the Immortal.

412 Him I call indeed a Brâhmana who in this world has risen above both ties, good and evil, who is free from grief, from sin, and from impurity.

413 Him I call indeed a Brâhmana who is bright like the moon, pure, serene, undisturbed, and in whom all gaiety is extinct.

414 Him I call indeed a Brâhmana who has traversed this miry road, the impassable world, difficult to pass, and its vanity, who has gone through, and reached the other shore, is thoughtful, steadfast, free from doubts, free from attachment, and content.

415 Him I call indeed a Brâhmana who in this world, having abandoned all desires, travels about without a home, and in whom all concupiscence is extinct.

416 Him I call indeed a Brâhma*n*a who, having abandoned all longings, travels about without a home, and in whom all covetousness is extinct.

417 Him I call indeed a Brâhma*n*a who, after leaving all bondage to men, has risen above all bondage to the gods, and is free from all and every bondage.

418 Him I call indeed a Brâhma*n*a who has left what gives pleasure and what gives pain, who is cold, and free from all germs (of renewed life), the hero who has conquered all the worlds.

419 Him I call indeed a Brâhma*n*a who knows the destruction and the return of beings everywhere, who is free from bondage, welfaring (Sugata), and awakened (Buddha).

420 Him I call indeed a Brâhma*n*a whose path the gods do not know, nor spirits (Gandharvas), nor men, whose passions are extinct, and who is an Arhat (venerable).

421 Him I call indeed a Brâhma*n*a who calls nothing his own, whether it be before, behind, or between, who is poor, and free from the love of the world.

422 Him I call indeed a Brâhmana, the manly, the noble, the hero, the great sage, the conqueror, the indifferent, the accomplished, the awakened.

423 Him I call indeed a Brâhmana who knows his former abodes, who sees heaven and hell, has reached the end of births, is perfect in knowledge, a sage, and whose perfections are all perfect.

NOTES

CHAPTER I

1 Dharma, though clear in its meaning, is difficult
to translate. It has different meanings in different
systems of philosophy, and its peculiar application
in the phraseology of Buddhism has been fully
elucidated by Burnouf, Introduction à l'Histoire
du Buddhisme, p. 41 seq. He writes: 'Je traduis
ordinairement ce terme par condition, d'autres
fois par lois, mais aucune de ces traductions n'est
parfaitement complète; il faut entendre par dharma
ce qui fait qu'une chose est ce qu'elle est, ce qui
constitue sa nature propre, comme l'a bien montré
Lassen, à l'occasion de la célèbre formule, "Ye
dharmâ betuprabhavâ." ' Etymologically the Latin
for-ma expresses the same general idea which was
expressed by dhar-ma. See also Burnouf, Lotus de
la bonne Loi, p. 524. Fausböll translates: 'Naturae
a mente principium ducunt,' which shows that
he rightly understood dharma in the Buddhist
sense. Gogerly (see Spence Hardy, Eastern

Monachism, p. 28) translates: 'Mind precedes action,' which, if not wrong, is at all events wrongly expressed; while Professor Weber's rendering, 'Die Pflichten aus dem Herz folgern,' is not admissible. D'Alwis (Buddhist Nirvâna, p. 70 seq.), following the commentary, proposes to give a more technical interpretation of this verse, viz. 'Mind is the leader of all its faculties. Mind is the chief (of all its faculties). The very mind is made up of those (faculties). If one speaks or acts with a polluted mind, then affliction follows him as the wheel follows the feet of the bearer (the bullock).' To me this technical acceptation seems not applicable here, where we have to deal with the simplest moral precepts, and not with psychological niceties of Buddhist philosophy. It should be stated, however, that Childers, who first (s.v. dhamma) approved of my translation, seems afterwards to have changed his opinion. On p. 120 of his excellent Pâli Dictionary he said: 'Three of the five khandhas, viz. vedanâ, saññâ, and saṅkhâra, are collectively termed dhammâ (plur.), "mental faculties," and in the first verse of Dhammapada the commentator takes the word dhammâ to mean those three faculties. But this interpretation appears forced and unnatural, and I look upon Dr. Max Müller's translation, "All that

we are is the result of what we have thought,"
as the best possible rendering of the spirit of the
phrase mano pubbaṅgamā dhammā.' But on p.
577 the same scholar writes: 'Of the four mental
khandhas the superiority of viññāna is strongly
asserted in the first verse of Dhammapada, "The
mental faculties (vedanā, saññā, and saṅkhāra) are
dominated by Mind, they are governed by Mind,
they are made up of Mind." That this is the true
meaning of the passage I am now convinced; see
D'Alwis, Nirvâna, pp. 70–75.' I do not deny that
this may have been the traditional interpretation,
at all events since the days of Buddhaghosa,
but the very legend quoted by Buddhaghosa in
illustration of this verse shows that its simpler
and purely moral interpretation was likewise
supported by tradition, and I therefore adhere to
my original translation. See also v. 109.

2 See Beal, Dhammapada, p. 169.

3 On akkokkhi, see Kakkâyana VI, 4, 17. D'Alwis,
Pâli Grammar, p. 38 note. 'When akkokkhi means
"he abused," it is derived from krus, not from
krudh.' See Senart, Kakkâyana, l. c.

On upanayhati=upanandhati, see J. P. T. S. 1887,
p. 126; it would mean literally he who ties up
such thoughts, that is he who holds fast to them.

5 Sanantana, translated by Childers by 'perpetual,
ancient, primeval,' cf. Sk. sana, sanâ, sanât,
sanâtana. Buddhaghosa explains it by porânaka.

6 Pare is explained by 'fools,' but it has that
meaning by implication only. It is οι πολλοί, cf,
Vinaya, ed. Oldenberg, vol. i, p. 5, l. 4. Yamâmase,
a 1 pers. plur. imp. Âtm., but really a Let in
Pâli. See Fausböll, Five Gâtakas, p. 38. Weber
translates, 'Wir sollen uns bezähmen hier,' which
may be right, but differs from Buddhaghosa.

7 Mâra must be taken in the Buddhist sense
of 'tempter,' or 'evil spirit.' See Burnouf,
Introduction, p. 76: 'Mâra est le démon de
l'amour, du péché et de la mort; c'est le tentateur
et l'ennemi de Buddha.' As to the definite
meaning of vîrya, see Burnouf, Lotus, p. 548.

In the Buddhistical Sanskrit, kusîda, 'idle,' is the
exact counterpart of the Pâli kusîta; see Burnouf,
Lotus, p. 548. On the change of Sanskrit d into Pâli
t, see Kuhn, Beiträge zur Pali Grammatik, p. 40;
Weber, Ind. Studien, XIII, p. 135.

9 The dark yellow dress, the Kâsâva or Kâshâya,
   is the distinctive garment of the Buddhist
   priests. See Vishnu-sûtra LXIII, 36. The play on
   the words anikkasâvo kâsâvam, or in Sanskrit
   anishkashâyah kâshâyam, cannot be rendered in
   English. Kashâya means 'impurity,' nish-kashâya,
   'free from impurity,' anish-kashâya, 'not free
   from impurity,' while kâshâya is the name of the
   yellowish Buddhist garment. The pun is evidently
   a favourite one, for, as Fausböll shows, it occurs
   also in the Mahâbhârata, XII, 568:

   Anishkashâye kâshâyam îhârtham iti viddhi
   tam, Dharmadhvagânâm mundânâm vrittyartham
   iti me matih.

   'Know that this yellow-coloured garment on a
   man who is not free from impurity, serves only
   for the purpose of cupidity; my opinion is, that
   it is meant to supply the means of living to those
   shavelings, who carry their virtue or the dharma
   like a flag.'

   (I read vrittyartham, according to the Bombay
   edition, instead of kritârtham, the reading of the
   Calcutta edition.)

   On the exact colour of the dress, see Bishop
   Bigandet, The Life or Legend of Gaudama, the

Budha of the Burmese, Rangoon, 1866, p. 504. Cf. *Gâtaka*, vol. ii, p. 198.

10 With regard to sîla, 'virtue,' see Burnouf, Lotus, p. 547.

11, 12 Sâra, which I have translated by 'truth,' has many meanings in Sanskrit. It means the sap of a thing, then essence or reality; in a metaphysical sense, the highest reality; in a moral sense, truth. It is impossible in a translation to do more than indicate the meaning of such words, and in order to understand them fully, we must know not only their definition, but their history. See Beal, Dhammapada, p. 64.

13 See Beal, Dhammapada, p. 65.

15 Killit*tha* is klis*ta*, a participle of klis. It means literally, what is spoilt. The abstract noun klesa, 'evil or sin,' is constantly employed in Buddhist works; see Burnouf, Lotus, p. 443.

16 Like klish*ta* in the preceding verse, visuddhi in the present has a technical meaning. One of Buddhaghosa's most famous works is called Visuddhi-magga. See Burnouf, Lotus, p. 844; Beal, Dhammapada, p. 67.

17, 18 'The evil path and the good path' are technical expressions for the descending and ascending scale of worlds through which all beings have to travel upward or downward, according to their deeds; see Bigandet, Life of Gaudama, p. 5, note 4, and p. 449; Burnouf, Introduction, p. 599; Lotus, p. 865, 1. 7; 1. 11. Fausböll translates 'heaven and hell,' which comes to the same; cf. vv. 126, 306.

19 In taking sahitam in the sense of samhitam or samhitâ, I follow the commentator who says, Tepitakassa Buddhavakanass' etam nâmam, but I cannot find another passage where the Tipitaka, or any portion of it, is called Sahita. Samhita in vv. 100–102 has a different meaning. The fact that some followers of Buddha were allowed to learn short portions only of the sacred writings by heart, and to repeat them, while others had to learn a larger collection, is shown by the story of Kakkhupâla, p. 3, of Mahâkâla, p. 26, &c. See Childers, s.v. sahita.

20 Sâmañña, which I have rendered by 'priesthood,' expresses all that belongs to, or constitutes a real Samana or Sramana, this being the Buddhist name corresponding to the Brâhmana, or priest, of the orthodox Hindus. Buddha himself is frequently called the Good Samana. Fausböll takes the abstract

word sâmañña as corresponding to the Sanskrit
sâmânya, 'community,' but Weber has well shown
that it ought to be taken as representing *sramanya*.
He might have quoted the Sâmañña-phala-sutta,
of which Burnouf has given such interesting
details in his Lotus, p. 449 seq. Fausböll also, in
his notes on v. 332, rightly explains sâmaññatâ by
sramanyatâ. See Childers, s.v. sâmañña.

Anupâdiyâno, which I have translated by
'caring for nothing,' has a technical meaning. It
is the negative of the fourth Nidâna, the so-called
Upâdâna, which Köppen has well explained by
Anhänghchkeit, 'clinging to the world, loving the
world.' Köppen, Die Religion des Buddha, p. 610.
Cf. Suttanipâta, v. 470.

On huram, see J. P. T. S., 1884, p. 103 seq.

CHAPTER II

*There is nothing in the tenth section of the
Dhammapada, as translated by Beal, corresponding to the verses of this chapter.

21 Apramâda, which Fausböll translates by
'vigilantia,' Gogerly by 'religion,' Childers by

'diligence,' expresses literally the absence of that giddiness or thoughtlessness which characterizes the state of mind of worldly people. It is the first entering into oneself, and hence all virtues are said to have their root in apramâda. (Ye keki kusalâ dhammâ sabbe te appamâdamûlakâ.) I have translated it by 'earnestness,' sometimes by 'reflection.' 'Immortality,' amrita, is explained by Buddhaghosa as Nirvâna. Amrita is used, no doubt, as a synonym of Nirvâna, but this very fact shows how many different conceptions entered from the very first into the Nirvâna of the Buddhists. See Childers, s.v. nibbâna, p. 269.

This verse, as recited to Asoka, occurs in the Dîpavamsa VI, 53, and in the Mahâvamsa, p. 25. See also Sanatsugâtîya, translated by Telang, Sacred Books of the East, vol. viii, p. 138.

22 The Ariyas, the noble or elect, are those who have entered on the path that leads to Nirvâna; see Köppen, p. 396. Their knowledge and general status is fully described; see Köppen, p. 436.

23 Childers, s.v. nibbâna, thinks that nibbâna here and in many other places means Arhatship.

25 Childers explains this island again as the state of an Arhat (arahatta-phalam).

28 Cf. Childers, Dictionary, Preface, p. xiv. See Vinaya, ed. Oldenberg, vol. i, p. 5, s. f.

31 Instead of saham, which Dr. Fausböll translates by 'vincens,' Dr. Weber by 'conquering.' I think we ought to read dahan, 'burning,' which was evidently the reading adopted by Buddhaghosa. Mr. R. C. Childers, whom I requested to see whether the MS. at the India Office gives saham or daham, writes that the reading daham is as clear as possible in that MS. Prof. Fausböll also now writes that my conjecture is confirmed by his own MSS. also. Mr. Neumann, however, retains saham. The fetters are meant for the senses. See verse 370.

32 See Childers, Notes, p. 5.

CHAPTER III

33 Kitta, here translated by thought, may be rendered also by mind or heart. It is, however, incorporeal, dwells in the heart, and is opposed

to the body, see Ab. 152, 338. Cf. *Gâtaka*, vol. i,
p. 400.

34 On Mâra, see verses 7 and 8.

35–39 Cf. *Gâtaka*, vol. i, pp. 312, 400.

39 Fausböll traces anavassuta, 'dissipated,' back to
the Sanskrit root syai, 'to become rigid;' but the
participle of that root would be *sîta*, not *syuta*.
Professor Weber suggests that anavassuta stands
for the Sanskrit anavasruta, which he translates
unbefleckt, 'unspotted.' If avasruta were the
right word, it might be taken in the sense of
'not fallen off, not fallen away,' but it could not
mean 'unspotted;' cf. dhairya*m* no susruvat, 'our
firmness ran away.' I have little doubt, however,
that avassuta represents the Sanskrit ava*s*ruta,
and is derived from the root sru, here used in
its technical sense, peculiar to the Buddhist
literature, and so well explained by Burnouf in
his Appendix XIV (Lotus, p. 820). He shows that,
according to Hema*k*andra and the *G*ina-ala*n*kâra,
âsravakshaya, Pâli âsavasa*m*khaya is counted as
the sixth abhi*g*ñâ, wherever six of these intellec-
tual powers are mentioned, instead of five. The
Chinese translate the term in their own Chinese

fashion by 'stillationis finis,' but Burnouf claims
for it the definite sense of destruction of faults or
vices. He quotes from the Lalita-vistara (Adhyâya
XXII, ed. Râjendra Lal Mittra, p. 448) the words
uttered by Buddha when he arrived at his
complete Buddhahood:—

> Sushkâ âsravâ na punah sravanti,
> 'The vices are dried up, they will not flow
> again;'

and he shows that the Pâli Dictionary, the
Abhidhânappadîpikâ, explains âsava simply
by kâma, 'love, pleasure of the senses.' In the
Mahâparinibbâna-sutta, three classes of âsava are
distinguished, the kâmâsavâ, the bhavâsavâ, and
the aviggâsavâ. See also Burnouf, Lotus, p. 665;
Childers, s.v. âsavo.

That sru means 'to run,' and is in fact a merely
dialectic variety of sru, has been proved by
Burnouf, while Boehtlingk thinks the substitu-
tion of s for s is a mistake. Âsrava therefore, or
âsrava, meant originally 'the running out towards
objects of the senses' (cf. sanga, âlaya, &c.), and
had nothing to do with âsrâva, 'a running, a
sore,' Atharva-veda I, 2, 4. This conception of the

original purport of â + sru or ava-sru is confirmed
by a statement of Colebrooke's, who, when
treating of the Gainas, writes (Miscellaneous
Essays, I, 382): 'Âsrava is that which directs
the embodied spirit (âsravayati purusham)
towards external objects. It is the occupation and
employment (vritti or pravritti) of the senses or
organs on sensible objects. Through the means of
the senses it affects the embodied spirit with the
sentiment of taction, colour, smell, and taste. Or it
is the association or connection of body with right
and wrong deeds. It comprises all the karmas, for
they (âsravayanti) pervade, influence, and attend
the doer, following him or attaching to him. It is a
misdirection (mithyâ-pravritti) of the organs, for it
is vain, a cause of disappointment, rendering the
organs of sense and sensible objects subservient
to fruition. Samvara is that which stops
(samvrinoti) the course of the foregoing, or closes
up the door or passage to it, and consists in
self-command or restraint of organs internal and
external, embracing all means of self-control and
subjection of the senses, calming and subduing
them.'

For a full account of the âsravas, see Lalita-
vistara, ed. Calc. pp. 445 and 552, where

Kshînâsrava is given as a name of Buddha. Âsrâva occurs in Âpastamba's Dharma sûtras II, 5, 9, where the commentator explains it by objects of the senses, by which the soul is made to run out. It is better, however, to take âsrâva here, too, as the act of running out, the affections, appetites, passions.

40 Anivesana has no doubt a technical meaning, and may signify, one who has left his house, his family and friends, to become a monk. A monk shall not return to his home, but travel about; he shall be anivesana, 'homeless,' anâgâra, 'houseless.' But I doubt whether this can be the meaning of anivesana here, as the sentence, let him be an anchorite, would come in too abruptly. I translate it therefore in a more general sense, let him not return or turn away from the battle, let him watch Mâra, even after he is vanquished, let him keep up a constant fight against the adversary, without being attached to anything or anybody.

43 See Beal, Dhammapada, p. 73.

CHAPTER IV

*See Beal, Dhammapada, p. 75.

44, 45 If I differ from the translation of Fausböll and
Weber, it is because the commentary takes the
two verbs, vigessati and pakessati, to mean in the
end the same thing, i.e. sakkhi-karissati, 'he will
perceive.' I have not ventured to take vigessate
for viganissati, though it should be remembered
that the overcoming of the earth and of the worlds
below and above, as here alluded to, is meant to
be achieved by means of knowledge. Pakessati,
'he will gather' (of. vi-ki, Indische Sprüche, 4560),
means also, like 'to gather' in English, 'he will
perceive or understand,' and the dhammapada,
or 'path of virtue,' is distinctly explained by
Buddhaghosa as consisting of the thirty-sev-
en states or stations which lead to Bodhi. (See
Burnouf, Lotus, p. 430; Hardy, Manual, p. 497.)
Dhammapada might, no doubt, mean also 'a law-
verse,' and sudesita, 'well taught,' and this double
meaning may be intentional here as elsewhere.
Buddha himself is called Mârga-darsaka and
Mârga-desika (cf. Lal. Vist. p. 551). There is a
curious similarity between these verses and verses
6540–41, and 9939 of the Sântiparva:

Pushpânîva vikinvantam anyatragatamanasam,
Anavâpteshu kâmeshu mrityur abhy〈 〉
mânavam〈 〉

'Death approaches man like one who is gathering
flowers, and whose mind is turned elsewhere,
before his desires have been fulfilled.'

Suptam vyâghram mahaugho vâ mrityur âdâya
gakkhati,
Sañkinvânakam evainam kâmânâm avitriptikam.

'As a stream (carries off) a sleeping tiger, death
carries off this man who is gathering flowers, and
who is not satiated in his pleasures.'

This last verse, particularly, seems to me clearly
a translation from Pâli, and the kam of sañkinvânakam looks as if put in metri causâ. See also
verse 12063.

46 The flower-arrows of Mâra, the tempter, are
borrowed from Kâma, the Hindu god of love. For
a similar expression see Lalita-vistara, ed. Calc.
p. 40, l. 20, mâyâmarîkisadrisâ vidyutphenopamâs
kapalâh. It is on account of this parallel passage
that I prefer to translate marîki by 'mirage,' and
not by 'sunbeam,' as Fausböll, or by 'solar atom,'
as Weber proposes. The expression, 'he will

never see the king of death,' is supposed to mean Arhatship by Childers, s.v. nibbâna, p. 270.

47 See Thiessen, Die Legende von Kisâgotamî, p. 9.

48 Antaka, 'death,' is given as an explanation of Mâra in the Amarakosha and Abhidhânappadîpika (cf. Fausböll, p. 210).

49 See Beal, Catena, p. 159, where vv. 49 and 50 are ascribed to Wessabhu, i.e. Visvabhû. See also Der Weise und der Thor, p. 134.

See Fausböll, Nogle Bemerkninger. Buddhaghosa renders ahe*th*ayam by avinâsento; and Kern, Verhandelingen der Koninkligke Akademie, Amsterdam, 1888, p. 19.

51 St. Matthew xxiii. 3, 'For they say, and do not.'

54 Tagara, a plant from which a scented powder is made. Mallaka or mallikâ, according to Benfey, is an oil vessel. Hence tagaramallikâ was supposed to mean a bottle holding aromatic powder, or oil made of the Tagara. Mallikâ, however, is given by Dr. Eitel (Handbook of Chinese Buddhism) as the name of a flower now called Casturi (musk) on account of its rich odour, and Dr. Morris informs me that he has found mallikâ in Pâli as a name of

THE DHAMMAPADA

jasmine. See also Childers, s.v.; Notes, p. 6; and
Beal, Dhammapada, p. 76.

58, 59 Cf. Beal, Dhammapada, p. 76.

CHAPTER V

60 'Life,' samsâra, is the constant revolution of
birth and death which goes on for ever until
the knowledge of the true law or the true
doctrine of Buddha enables a man to free himself
from samsâra, and to enter into Nirvâna. See
Buddhaghosha's Parables, Parable XIX, p. 134.

61 Cf. Suttanipâta, v. 46.

63 Cf. Beal, Dhammapada, p. 77.

64 The same verses occur in the Mahâbh. Sauptikap.
v. 178; see also Sabhâp. v. 1945.

65 Cf. Beal, Dhammapada, p. 78.

67 See Beal, l.c. p. 78.

69 Taken from the Samyutta-nikâya, where,
however, we read thânanhi instead of madhuvâ;
see Feer, Comptes Rendus, 1871, p. 64.

70 The commentator clearly takes saṅkhâta in the sense of saṅkhyâta, 'reckoned,' for he explains it by ñâtadhammâ, tulitadhammâ. The eating with the tip of Kusa grass has reference to the fastings performed by the Brâhmans, but disapproved of, except as a moderate discipline, by the followers of Buddha. This verse seems to interrupt the continuity of the other verses which treat of the reward of evil deeds, or of the slow but sure ripening of every sinful act. See Childers, s.v. saṅkhâto.

71 I am not at all certain of the simile, unless mukkati, as applied to milk, can be used in the sense of changing or turning sour. In Manu IV, 172, where a similar sentence occurs, the commentators are equally doubtful: Nâdharmas karito loke sadyah phalati gaur iva, 'for an evil act committed in the world does not bear fruit at once, like a cow;' or 'like the earth (in due season);' or 'like milk.' See Childers, Notes, p. 6.

72 I take ñattam for gñapitam, the causative of gñâtam, for which in Sanskrit, too, we have the form without i, gñaptam. This gñaptam, 'made known, revealed,' stands in opposition to the khanna, 'covered, hid,' of the preceding verse.

Sukkamsa, which Fausböll explains by sultlamsa, has probably a more technical and special meaning. Childers traces ñattam to the Vedic gñâtram, 'knowledge.' Fausböll refers to Gâtaka, vol. i, p. 445, v. 118.

75 Viveka, which in Sanskrit means chiefly understanding, has several meanings with the Buddhists, and among them the more technical meaning of separation, whether separation from the world and retirement to the solitude of the forest (kâya-viveka), or separation from idle thoughts (kitta-viveka), or the highest separation and freedom (Nirvâna). As true knowledge cannot be said to be a road to wealth, I have taken añña, not for âgñâ, but for anyâ.

CHAPTER VI

78 It is hardly possible to take mitte kalyâne in the technical sense of kalyâna-mitra, 'ein geistlicher Rath,' a spiritual guide. Burnouf (Introd. p. 284) shows that in the technical sense kalyâna-mitra was widely spread in the Buddhist world.

79 Ariya, 'elect, venerable,' is explained by the commentator as referring to Buddha and other teachers.

80 See verses 33 and 145, the latter being a mere repetition of our verse. The nettikâs, to judge from the commentary and from the general purport of the verse, are not simply water-carriers, but builders of canals and aqueducts, who force the water to go over the fields where it would not go by itself. The Chinese translator says, 'the pilot manages his ship.' See Beal, l.c. p. 79.

83 The first line is very doubtful. Mr. Childers writes, 'I think it will be necessary to take sabbattha in the sense of "everywhere," or "under all circumstances;" pañkakhandâdibhedesu, sabba-dhammesu, says Buddhaghosa. I do not think we need assume that B. means the word vigahanti to be a synonym of vaganti. I would rather take the whole sentence together as a gloss upon the word vaganti:—vagantîti arahattaññânena apakaddhantâ khandarâgam vigahanti; vaganti means that, ridding themselves of lust by the wisdom which Arhatship confers, they cast it away.' The line means 'the righteous walk on (unmoved) in all the conditions of life.' Nindâ, pasamsâ, sukha, dukkha are four of the eight lokadhammas, or earthly conditions; the remaining lokadhammas are lâbha, alâbha, yasa, ayasa, I have adopted the translation of W. Morris, see Journal of P.T.S., 1891–93, p. 41.

In v. 245, passatâ, 'by a man who sees,' means 'by a man who sees clearly or truly.' In the same manner vrag may mean, not simply 'to walk,' but 'to walk properly,' or may be used synonymously with pravrag.

84 That the last line forms the apodosis is shown by the demonstrative pronoun sa.

85 'The other shore' is meant for Nirvâna, 'this shore' for common life. On reaching Nirvâna, the dominion of death is overcome. The commentator supplies târitvâ, 'having crossed,' in order to explain the accusative makkudheyyam, but possibly pâram essanti should here be taken as one word, in the sense of overcoming.

87, 88 Dark and bright are meant for bad and good; cf. Suttanipâta, v. 526, and Dhp. v. 167. Leaving one's home is the same as becoming a mendicant, without a home or family, an anâgâra, or anchorite. A man in that state of viveka, or retirement (see v. 75, note), sees, that where

before there seemed to be no pleasure there real
pleasure is to be found, or vice versâ. A similar
idea is expressed in verse 99. See Burnouf, Lotus,
p. 474, where he speaks of 'Le plaisir de la satisfaction, né de la distinction.' On pariyodapeyya,
see Childers, s.v.

The five troubles or evils of the mind are
passion, anger, ignorance, arrogance, pride; see
Burnouf, Lotus, pp. 360, 443. As to pariyodapeyya, see verse 183, and Lotus, pp. 523, 528; as to
akiñkano, see Mahâbh. XII, 6568, 1240.

89 The elements of knowledge are the seven
Sambodhyaṅgas, on which see Burnouf, Lotus,
p. 796. D'Alwis explains them as the thirty-seven
Bodhipakkhiya-dhammâ. Khînâsavâ, which I have
translated by 'they whose frailties have been
conquered,' may also be taken in a more metaphysical sense, as explained in the note to v. 39.
The same applies to the other terms occurring in
this verse, such as âdâna, anupâdâya, &c.
Dr. Fausböll seems inclined to take âsava in this
passage, and in the other passages where it occurs,
as the Pâli representative of âsraya. But âsraya,
in Buddhist phraseology, means rather the five
organs of sense with manas, 'the soul,' and these
are kept distinct from the âsavas, 'the inclinations,

the appetites, passions, or vices.' The commentary
on the Abhidharma, when speaking of the
Yogâkâras, says, 'En réunissant ensemble les
réceptacles (âsraya), les choses reçues (âsrita) et
les supports (âlambana), qui sont chacun composés
de six termes, on a dix-huit termes qu'on appelle
"Dhâtus" ou contenants. La collection des six
réceptacles, ce sont les organes de la vue, de
l'ouïe, de l'odorat, du goût, du toucher, et le
"manas" (ou l'organe du cœur), qui est le dernier.
La collection des six choses reçues, c'est la connaissance produite par la vue et par les autres sens
jusqu'au "manas" inclusivement. La collection des
six supports, ce sont la forme et les autres attributs
sensibles jusqu'au "Dharma" (la loi ou l'être)
inclusivement.' See Burnouf, Introduction, p. 449.

Parinibbuta is again a technical term, the
Sanskrit parinivrita meaning 'freed from all
worldly fetters,' like vimukta. See Burnouf,
Introduction, p. 590. See Childers, s.v. nibbâna,
p. 270, and Notes on Dhammapada, p. 3; and
D'Alwis, Buddhist Nirvâna, p. 75.

CHAPTER VII

91 Satîmanto, Sanskrit smritimantah, 'possessed of
memory, but here used in the technical sense of
sati, the first of the Bodhyaṅgas. See Burnouf,
Introduction, p. 797. Clough translates it by
'intense thought,' and this is the original meaning
of smar, even in Sanskrit. See Lectures on the
Science of Language, vol. ii, p. 332.

Uyyuñganti, which Buddhaghosa explains by
'they exert themselves,' may possibly signify 'they
depart,' i.e. they leave their family, and embrace
an ascetic life. See note to verse 235. See also Rhys
Davids, Mahâparinibbâna-sutta, Sacred Books of
the East, vol. xi, p. 22.

92 Suññato and animitto are adjectives belonging to
vimokho, one of the many names of Nirvâna, or,
according to Childers, s.v. nibbâna, p. 270,
Arhatship; see Burnouf, Introduction, pp. 442,
462, on sûnya. The Sanskrit expression sûn-
yatânimittâpranihitam occurs in L'enfant egaré, 5 a,
l. 4. Nimitta is cause in the most general sense, i.e.
what causes existence. The commentator explains
it chiefly in a moral sense: Râgâdinimittâbhâvena
animittam, tehi ka vimuttan ti animitto vimokho,
i.e. owing to the absence of passion and other

causes, without causation; because freed from
these causes, therefore it is called freedom
without causation. See Childers, Pâli Dictionary,
p. 270, col. 2, line 1.

The simile is intended to compare the ways of
those who have obtained spiritual freedom to the
flight of birds, it being difficult to understand
how the birds move on without putting their feet
on anything. This, at least, is the explanation
of the commentator. The same metaphor occurs
Mahâbh. XII, 6763. Childers translates, 'leaving
no more trace of existence than a bird in the air.'

95 Without the hints given by the commentator,
we should probably take the three similes of this
verse in their natural sense, as illustrating the
imperturbable state of an Arahanta, or venerable
person. The earth is always represented as an
emblem of patience; the bolt of Indra, if taken
in its technical sense, as the bolt of a gate, might
likewise suggest the idea of firmness; while the
lake is a constant representative of serenity and
purity. The commentator, however, suggests that
what is meant is, that the earth, though flowers are
cast on it, does not feel pleasure, nor a door-step
displeasure, although less savoury things are

thrown upon it; and that in like manner a wise person is indifferent to honour and dishonour.

96 That this very natural threefold division, thought, word, and deed, the trividha-dvâra or the three doors of the Buddhists (Hardy, Manual. p. 494), was not peculiar to the Buddhists or unknown to the Brâhmans, has been proved against Dr. Weber by Professor Köppen in his 'Religion des Buddha,' I, p. 445. He particularly called attention to Manu XII, 4–8; and he might have added Mahâbh. XII, 4059, 6512, 6549, 6554; XIII, 5677, &c. Dr. Weber has himself afterwards brought forward a passage from the Atharvaveda, VI, 96, 3 (yak kakshushâ manasâ yak ka vâkâ upârima), which, however, has a different meaning. A better one was quoted by him from the Taitt. Âr. X, 1, 12 (yan me manasâ, vâkâ, karmanâ vâ dushkritam kritam). Similar expressions have been shown to exist in the Zend-avesta, and among the Manichæans (Lassen, Indische Alterthumskunde, III, p. 414; see also Boehtlingk's Dictionary, s. v. kâya, and Childers, s.v. kâyo). There was no ground, therefore, for supposing that this formula had found its way into the Christian liturgy from Persia, for, as Professor Cowell remarks (Journal of Philology, vol. iii, p. 215), Greek writers, such as Plato, employ very

similar expressions, e.g. Protag. p. 348, 30, πρὸς ἅπαν ἔργον καὶ λόγον καὶ διανόημα. In fact, the opposition between words and deeds occurs in almost every writer, from Homer downwards; and the further distinction between thoughts and words is clearly implied even in such expressions as, 'they say in their heart.' That the idea of sin being committed by thought was not a new idea, even to the Jews, may be seen from Prov. xxiv. 9, 'the thought of foolishness is sin.' In the Âpastamba-sûtras, lately edited by Professor Bühler, we find the expression, atho yatkiñka manasâ vâkâ kakshushâ vâ saṅkalpayan dhyâyaty âhâbhivipasyati vâ tathaiva tad bhavatîtyupadis-anti, 'they say that whatever a Brahman intending with his mind, voice, or eye, thinks, says, or looks, that will be.' This is clearly a very different division, and it is the same which is intended in the passage from the Atharva-veda, quoted above. In the mischief done by the eye, we have, perhaps, the first indication of the evil eye. (Mahâbh. XII, 3417. See Dhammapada, vv. 231–234, and Nâgârguna's Suhrillekha.)

On the technical meaning of tâdi, see Childers, s.v. D'Alwis (p. 78) has evidently received the right interpretation, but has not understood it.

Mâd*ris*a also is used very much like tâd*ris*a, and from it mâriso, a venerable person, in Sanskrit mârsha.

98 See Childers, s.v. ninna*m*.

CHAPTER VIII

100 This Sahasravarga, or Chapter of the Thousands, is quoted by that name in the Mahâvastu (Minayeff, Mélanges Asiatiques, VI, p. 583): Teshâm Bhagavâñ *g*atilânâ*m* Dharmapadeshu sahasravarga*m* bhâshati: 'Sahasram api vâ*k*ânâm anarthapadasa*m*hitânâm, ekârthavatî *s*reyâ yâ*m* *s*rutvâ upasâmyati. Sahasram api gâthânâm anarthapadasa*m*hitânâm, ekârthavatî *s*reyâ yâ*m* *s*rutvâ upasâmyati' (MS. R. A. S. Lond.) Here the Pâli text seems decidedly more original and perfect.

104 Gita*m*, according to the commentator, stands for *g*ito (li*n*gavipallâso, i.e. viparyâsa); see also Senart in Journal Asiatique, 1880, p. 500.

The Devas (gods), Gandharvas (fairies), and other fanciful beings of the Brahmanic religion, such as

the Nâgas, Sarpas, Garu*d*as, &c., were allowed to
continue in the traditional language of the people
who had embraced Buddhism. See the pertinent
remarks of Burnouf, Introduction, pp. 134 seq.,
184. On Mâra, the tempter, see v. 7. Sâstram
Aiyar, On the *G*aina Religion, p. xx, says:
'Moreover as it is declared in the *G*aina Vedas
that all the gods worshipped by the various
Hindu sects, viz. *S*iva, Brahma, Vishnu, Ga*n*apati,
Subramaniyan, and others, were devoted
adherents of the above-mentioned Tîrthaṅkaras,
the *G*ainas therefore do not consider them as
unworthy of their worship; but as they are
servants of Arugan, they consider them to be
deities of their system, and accordingly perform
certain pûgâs in honour of them, and worship
them also.' The case is more doubtful with
orthodox Buddhists.

'Orthodox Buddhists,' as Mr. D'Alwis writes
(Attanagalu-vansa, p. 55), 'do not consider the
worship of the Devas as being sanctioned by him
who disclaimed for himself and all the Devas any
power over man's soul. Yet the Buddhists are
everywhere idol-worshippers. Buddhism, however,
acknowledges the existence of some of the Hindu
deities, and from the various friendly offices

which those Devas are said to have rendered to
Gotama, Buddhists evince a respect for their idols.'
See also Buddhaghosha's Parables, p. 162.

109 Dr. Fausböll, in a most important note, called
attention to the fact that the same verse, with
slight variations, occurs in Manu. We there read,
II, 121:

Abhivâdanasîlasya nitya*m* v*ri*ddhopasevina*h*,
*K*atvâri sampravardhante âyur vidyâ yaso balam.

Here the four things are, life, knowledge, glory,
power.

In the Âpastamba-sûtras, I, 2, 5, 15, the reward
promised for the same virtue is svargam âyus *k*a,
'heaven and long life.' It seems, therefore, as if the
original idea of this verse came from the
Brahmans, and was afterwards adopted by the
Buddhists. See Mahâbh. V, 1398; Weber, Ind.
Stud. XIII, p. 405. How largely it spread is shown
by Dr. Fausböll from the Asiatic Researches, XX,
p. 259, where the same verse of the Dhammapada
is mentioned as being widely in use among the
Buddhists of Siam.

112 On kusîto, see note to verse 7.

CHAPTER IX

125 Cf. Suttanipâta, v. 661; Indische Sprüche, 1581, Kathâsaritsâgara, 49, 222.

126 For a description of hell and its long, yet not endless sufferings, see Buddhaghosha's Parables, p. 132. The pleasures of heaven, too, are frequently described in these Parables and elsewhere. Buddha himself enjoyed these pleasures of heaven, before he was born for the last time. It is probably when good and evil deeds are equally balanced, that men are born again as human beings; this, at least, is the opinion of the *Gainas*. Cf. Chintâma*n*i, ed. H. Bower, Introd, p. xv.

127 Cf. St. Luke xii. 2, 'For there is nothing covered that shall not be revealed;' and Psalm cxxxix. 8–12.

CHAPTER X

129 One feels tempted, no doubt, to take upama in the sense of 'the nearest (der Nächste), the neighbour,' and to translate, 'having made oneself one's

neighbour,' i.e. loving one's neighbour as oneself.
But as upamăm, with a short a, is the correct
accusative of upamâ, we must translate, 'having
made oneself the likeness, the image of others,
having placed oneself in the place of others.'
This is an expression which occurs frequently in
Sanskrit; cf. Hitopadesa I, ii:

Prânâ yathâtmano bhîshtâ bhûtânâm
    api te tathâ,
Âtmaupamyena bhûteshu dayâm kurvanti
    sâdhavah.

'As life is dear to oneself, it is dear also to other
living beings: by comparing oneself with others,
good people bestow pity on all beings.'

See also Hit. I, 12; Râm. V, 23, 5, âtmânam
upamâm kritvâ sveshu dâreshu ramyatâm,
'making oneself a likeness, i.e. putting oneself
in the position of other people, it is right to love
none but one's own wife.' Dr. Fausböll has called
attention to similar passages in the Mahâbhârata,
XIII, 5569 seq.

130 Cf. St. Luke vi. 31.

131 Dr. Fausböll points out the striking similarity
between this verse and two verses occurring in
Manu and the Mahâbhârata:—Manu V, 45:

> Yo himsakâni bhûtâni hinasty
> âtmasukhekkhayâ,
> Sa gîvams ka mritas kaiva na kvakit sukham
> edhate.
> Mahâbhârata XIII, 5568:

> Ahimsakâni bhûtâni dandena vinihanti yah,
> Âtmanah sukham ikkhan sa pretya naiva sukhî
> bhavet.

If it were not for ahimsakâni, in which Manu and
the Mahâbhârata agree, I should say that the
verses in both were Sanskrit modifications of the
Pâli original. The verse in the Mahâbhârata pre-
supposes the verse of the Dhammapada.

133 See Mahâbhârata XII, 4056.

134 See Childers, s.v. nibbâna, p. 270, and s.v. kâmso;
D'Alwis, Buddhist Nirvâna, p. 35.

136 The metaphor of 'burning' for 'suffering' is very
common in Buddhist literature. Everything burns,
i.e. everything suffers, was one of the first
experiences of Buddha himself. See v. 146.

138 'Cruel suffering' is explained by sîsaroga, 'headache,' &c. 'Loss' is taken for loss of money. 'Injury of the body' is held to be the cutting off of the arm, and other limbs. 'Heavy afflictions' are, again, various kinds of diseases.

139 Upasarga means 'accident, misfortune.' Dr. Fausböll translates râgato va upassaggam by 'fulgentis (lunae) defectionem;' Dr. Weber by 'Bestrafung vom König;' Beal by 'some governmental difficulty.' Abbhakkhânam, Sanskrit abhyâkhyânam, is a heavy accusation for high treason, or similar offences. Beal translates, 'some false accusation.' The 'destruction of pleasures or treasures' is explained by gold being changed to coals (see Buddhaghosha's Parables, p. 98; Thiessen, Kisâgotamî, p. 6), pearls to cotton seed, corn to potsherds, and by men and cattle becoming blind, lame, &c.

141 Cf. Hibbert Lectures, p. 355. Dr. Fausböll has pointed out that the same or a very similar verse occurs in a legend taken from the Divyâvadâna, and translated by Burnouf (Introduction, p. 313 seq.) Burnouf translates the verse: 'Ce n'est ni la coutume de marcher nu, ni les cheveux nattés, ni

l'usage d'argile, ni le choix des diverses especes
d'aliments, ni l'habitude de coucher sur la terre
nue, ni la poussière, ni la malpropreté, ni l'attention a fuir l'abri d'un toit, qui sont capables de
dissiper le trouble dans lequel nous jettent les
désirs non-satisfaits; mais qu'un homme, maître de
ses sens, calme, recueilli, chaste, évitant de faire
du mal à aucune créature, accomplisse la Loi, et il
sera, quoique paré d'ornements, un Brâhmane, un
Cramana, un Religieux.' See also Suttanipâta,
v. 248.

Walking naked and the other things mentioned
in our verse are outward signs of a saintly life,
and these Buddha rejects because they do not
calm the passions. Nakedness he seems to have
rejected on other grounds too, if we may judge
from the Sumâgadhâ-avadâna: 'A number of naked
friars were assembled in the house of the daughter
of Anâtha-pindika. She called her daughter-in-law,
Sumâgadhâ, and said, "Go and see those highly
respectable persons." Sumâgadhâ, expecting to see
some of the saints, like Sâriputra, Maudgalyâyana,
and others, ran out full of joy. But when she saw
these friars with their hair like pigeon wings,
covered by nothing but dirt, offensive, and
looking like demons, she became sad. "Why are

you sad?" said her mother-in-law. Sumâgadhâ replied, "O mother, if these are saints, what must sinners be like?" '

Burnouf (Introduction, p. 312) supposed that the *Gainas* only, and not the Buddhists, allowed nakedness. But the *Gainas*, too, do not allow it universally. They are divided into two parties, the *S*vetambaras and Digambaras. The *S*vetambaras, clad in white, are the followers of Par*s*vanâtha, and wear clothes. The Digambaras, i.e. sky-clad, disrobed, are followers of Mahâvîra, resident chiefly in Southern India. At present they, too, wear clothing, but not when eating. See Sâstram Aiyar, p. xxi.

The *g*atâ, or the hair platted and gathered up in a knot, was a sign of a *S*aiva ascetic. The sitting motionless is one of the postures assumed by ascetics. Clough explains ukku*t*ika as 'the act of sitting on the heels;' Wilson gives for utka*t*uk-âsana, 'sitting on the hams.' See Fausböll, note on verse 140.

142   This verse has to be taken in connection with the preceding verse, to show that though a man cares about his outward appearance and is well dressed, he may be a true disciple for all that, if only he

practises virtue. As to da*n*danidhâna, see Mahâbh XII, 6559, and Suttanipâta, v. 34.

145 The same as verse 80. According to Fausböll and Subhûti we ought to render the verses by, 'What man is there found on earth so restrained by shame that he never provokes reproof, as a good horse the whip?' See, however, Childers, s.v. appabodhati. Fausböll maintains his view.

CHAPTER XI

148 Dr. Fausböll informs me that Childers proposed the emendation mara*n*anta*m* hi gîvita*m*. The following extract from a letter, addressed by Childers to Dr. Fausböll, will be read with interest:—'As regards Dhp. v. 148, I have no doubt whatever. I quite agree with you that the idea (mors est vita ejus) is a profound and noble one, but the question is, Is the idea there? I think not. Mara*n*am tamhi gîvitam is not Pâli, I mean not a Pâli construction, and years ago even it grated on my ear as a harsh phrase. The reading of your MSS. of the texts is nothing; your MSS. of Dhammapada are very bad ones, and it is merely the vicious Sinhalese spelling of bad MSS., like

kamma*m*ta*m* for kammanta*m*. But the comment
sets the question at rest at once, for it explains
mara*n*anta*m* by mara*n*apariyosânam, which is
exactly the same. I see there is one serious
difficulty left, that all your MSS. seem to have
tamhi, and not ta*m* hi; but are you sure it is so?
There was a Dhammapada in the India Office
Library, and I had a great hunt for it a few days
ago, but to my deep disappointment it is missing.
I do not agree with you that the sentence "All Life
is bounded by Death," is trivial: it is a truism, but
half the noblest passages in poetry are truisms,
and unless I greatly mistake, this very passage
will be found in many other literatures.'

Dr. Fausböll adds:—

'I have still the same doubt as before, because
of all my MSS. reading mara*n*am tamhi. I do
not know the readings of the London MSS. The
explanation of the commentary does not settle
the question, as it may as well be considered an
explanation of my reading as of the reading
which Childers proposed.—V. FAUSBÖLL.'

Fausböll has now surrendered his doubts, and he
produces himself a number of passages where this
phrase mara*n*ânta*m* hi *g*îvanam occurs, e.g.

Mahâbh. (ed. Calcutta), XI, 48; 207; XII, 829;
Râmây. (ed. Bombay), Ayodhyâk., p. 197;
Divyâvadâna, p, 27; 100,

149 In the Rudrâyanâvadâna of the Divyâvadâna this
verse appears as,

Yânîmâny apariddhâni vikshiptâni diso disah,
Kapotavarnâny asthîni tâni drishtvaiha kâ ratih.

See Schiefner, Mél. Asiat. VIII, p. 589; Gâtaka,
vol. i, p. 322.

150 The expression mamsalohitalepanam is curiously
like the expression used in Manu VI, 76,
mâmsasonitalepanam, and in several passages of
the Mahâbhârata, XII, 12462, 12053, as pointed
out by Dr. Fausböll.

153, 154 These two verses are famous among
Buddhists, for they are the words which the
founder of Buddhism is supposed to have uttered
at the moment he attained to Buddhahood. (See
Spence Hardy, Manual, p. 180.) According to the
Lalita-vistara, however, the words uttered on that
solemn occasion were those quoted in the note to
verse 39. In the commentary on the Brahmagâla
this verse is called the first speech of Buddha, his

last speech being the words in the
Mahâparinibbâna-sutta, 'Life is subject to age;
strive in earnest, &c.' The words used in the
Mahâparinibbâna-sutta, Chap. IV, 2, *Katunnam
dhammânam ananubodhâ appativedhâ evam idam
dîgham addhânam sandhâvitam samsâritam
mamañ k' eva tumhâkañ ka*, answer to the antici-
pation expressed in our verse.

The exact rendering of this verse has been much
discussed, chiefly by Mr. D'Alwis in the
Attanugaluvansa, p. cxxviii, and again in his
Buddhist Nirvâna, p. 78; also by Childers, Notes
on Dhammapada, p. 4, and in his Dictionary.
Gogerly translated: 'Through various transmigrations I must travel, if I do not discover the
builder whom I seek.' Spence Hardy: 'Through
many different births I have run (to me not
having found), seeking the architect of the
desire-resembling house.' Fausböll: 'Multiplices
generationis revolutiones percurreram, non
inveniens, domus (corporis) fabricatorem
quaerens.' And again (p. 322): 'Multarum
generationum revolutio mihi subeunda esset,
nisi invenissem domus fabricatorem.' Childers:
'I have run through the revolution of countless
births, seeking the architect of this dwelling and

finding him not.' D'Alwis: 'Through transmigrations of numerous births have I run, not discovering, (though) seeking the house builder.' All depends on how we take sandhavissam, which Fausböll takes as a conditional, Childers, following Trenckner, as an aorist, because the sense imperatively requires an aorist. I had formerly translated it as a future, though qualifying it by the participle present anibbisan, i.e. not finding, and taking it in the sense of, if or so long as I do not find the true cause of existence. Anibbisan I had translated by not resting (anirvisan), but the commentator seems to authorise the meaning of not finding (avindanto, alabhanto), and in that case all the material difficulties of the verse seem to me to disappear.

'The maker of the tabernacle' is explained as a poetical expression for the cause of new births, at least according to the views of Buddha's followers, whatever his own views may have been. Buddha had conquered Mâra, the representative of worldly temptations, the father of worldly desires, and as desires (taṃhâ) are, by means of upâdâna and bhava, the cause of gâti, or 'birth,' the destruction of desires and the conquest of Mâra are nearly the same thing, though expressed differently in the philosophical and legendary language of the Buddhists. Ta*m*hâ, 'thirst' or 'craving,' is mentioned as serving in the army of Mâra. (Lotus, p. 443.)

155 On *ghâ*yanti, i.e. kshâyanti, see Dr. Bollensen's learned remarks, Zeitschrift der Deutschen Morgenl. Gesellschaft, XVIII, 834, and Boehtlingk-Roth, s.v. kshâ.

CHAPTER XII

157 The three watches of the night are meant for the three stages of life. Cf. St. Mark xiii. 37, 'And what I say unto you, I say unto all, Watch.'

158 Cf. *G*âtaka, vol. ii, p. 441.

161 The Chinese translation renders vagiram by 'steel drill.'

164 The reed either dies after it has borne fruit, or is cut down for the sake of its fruit.

Di*tth*i, literally 'view,' is used even by itself, like the Greek 'hairesis,' in the sense of heresy (see Burnouf, Lotus, p. 444). In other places a distinction is made between mi*kkh*âdi*tth*i (vv. 167, 316) and sammâdi*tthi* (v. 319). If arahata*m* ariyâna*m* are used in their technical sense, we should translate 'the reverend Arhats,'—Arhat being the highest degree of the four orders of Ariyas, viz. *S*rotaâpanna, Sakadâgâmin, Anâgâmin, and Arhat. See note to verse 178.

166 Attha, lit. 'object,' must here be taken in a moral sense, as 'duty' rather than as 'advantage.' Childers rendered it by 'spiritual good.' The story which Buddhaghosa tells of the Thera Attadattha gives a clue to the origin of some of his parables, which seem to have been invented to suit the text of the Dhammapada rather than vice versâ. A similar case occurs in the commentary to verse 227.

CHAPTER XIII

167 Childers says, I have not the slightest notion of the meaning of lokavaddhano. Could it mean, Do not swell the number of worldlings?

168, 169 See Rhys Davids, Buddhism, p. 65.

170 See Suttanipâta, v, 1118.

175 Hamsa may be meant for the bird, whether flamingo, or swan, or ibis (see Hardy, Manual, p. 17), but it may also, I believe, be taken in the sense of saint. As to iddhi, 'magical power,' i.e. riddhi, see Burnouf, Lotus, p. 310; Spence Hardy, Manual, pp. 498, 504; Legends, pp. 55, 177; and note to verse 254.

178 Sotâpatti, the technical term for the first step in the path that leads to Nirvâna. There are four such steps, or stages, and on entering each, a man receives a new title:—

(1) The Srotaâpanna, lit. he who has got into the stream. A man may have seven more births before he reaches the other shore, i.e. Nirvâna.

(2) Sakridâgâmin, lit. he who comes back once, so called because, after having entered this stage, a man is born only once more among men or gods. Childers shows that this involves really two more births, one in the deva world, the other in the world of men. Burnouf says the same, Introduction, p. 293.

(3) Anâgâmin, lit. he who does not come back, so called because, after this stage, a man cannot be born again in a lower world, but can only

be born into a Brahman world, before he
reaches Nirvâna.

(4) Arhat, the venerable, the perfect, who has
reached the highest stage that can be reached,
and from which Nirvâna is perceived
(sukkhavipassanâ, Lotus, p. 849). See Hardy,
Eastern Monachism, p. 280; Burnouf,
Introduction, p. 209; Köppen, p. 398; D'Alwis,
Attanugaluvansa, p. cxxiv; Feer, Sutra en 42
articles, p. 6.

CHAPTER XIV

179, 180 Buddha, the Awakened, is to be taken as an
appellative rather than as the proper name of the
Buddha (see v. 183). It means, anybody who has
arrived at complete knowledge. Anantagokaram
I take in the sense of, possessed of unlimited
knowledge. Apadam, which Dr. Fausböll takes
as an epithet of Buddha and translates by 'non
investigabilis,' is translated 'trackless,' in order to
show the play on the word pada; see Childers, s.v.
The commentator says: 'The man who is possessed
of even a single one of such conditions as râga,

&c., him ye may lead forward; but the Buddha has not even one condition or basis of renewed existence, and therefore by what track will you lead this unconditioned Buddha?' Cf. Dhp. vv. 92, 420; and *Gâtaka*, vol. i, pp. 79, 313.

182 Mr. Beal (Dhammapada, p. 110) states that this verse occurs also in the Sûtra of the forty-two sections.

183 This verse is again one of the most solemn verses among the Buddhists. According to Csoma Körösi, it ought to follow the famous Âryâ stanza, 'Ye dhammâ' (Lotus, p. 522), and serve as its complement. But though this may be the case in Tibet, it was not so originally. The same verse (ascribed to Kanakamuni) occurs at the end of the Chinese translation of the Prâtimoksha (Beal, J. R. A. S. XIX, p. 473; Catena, p. 159); in the Tibetan translation of the Gâthâsaṅgraha, v. 14 (Schiefner, Mél. Asiat. VIII, pp. 568, 586; and Csoma Körösi, As. Res. XX, p. 79). Burnouf has fully discussed the metre and meaning of our verse on pp. 527, 528 of his 'Lotus.' He prefers sa*k*ittaparidamanam, which Csoma translated by 'the mind must be brought under entire subjection' (sva*k*ittapari-damanam), and the late Dr. Mill by 'proprii intellectus subjugatio.' But his own MS. of the

Mahâpadhâna-sutta gave likewise sakittapariyoda-
panam, and this is no doubt the correct reading.
(See D'Alwis, Attanugaluvansa, p. cxxiv.) We
found pariyodapeyya in verse 88, in the sense of
purging oneself from the troubles of the mind.
From the same verb, (pari) ava + dai, we may
derive the name Avadâna, a legend, originally a
pure and virtuous act, an αρίστεια, 'afterwards a
sacred story, and possibly a story the hearing of
which purifies the mind. See Boehtlingk-Roth,
s.v. avadâna.

184 Childers, following the commentator, translates,
'Patience, which is long-suffering, is the best
devotion, the Buddhas declare that Nirvâna is the
best (of things).'

185 Pâtimokkhe, 'under the law,' i.e. according to the
law, the law which leads to Moksha, or 'freedom.'
Prâtimoksha is the title of the oldest collection
of the moral laws of the Buddhists (Burnouf,
Introduction, p. 300; Bigandet, The Life of
Gaudama, p. 439; Rhys Davids, Buddhism, p. 162),
and as it was common both to the Southern and
the Northern Buddhists, pâtimokkhe in our
passage may possibly be meant, as Professor
Weber suggests, as the title of that very collection.
The commentator explains it by getthakasîla and

pâtimokkhasîla. Sayanâsam might stand for
sayanâsanam, see Mahâbh. XII, 6684; but in
Buddhist literature it is intended for sayanâsanam;
see also Mahâbh. XII, 9978, sayyâsane.' Fausböll
now reads pântam instead of patthañ, as in
Suttanipâta, 337.

187 There is a curious similarity between this verse
and verse 6503 (9919) of the Sântiparva:

Yakka kâmasukham loke, yak ka divyam mahat
    sukham,
Trishnâkshayasukhasyaite nârhatah shodasîm
    kalâm.

'And whatever delight of love there is on earth,
and whatever is the great delight in heaven, they
are not worth the sixteenth part of the pleasure
which springs from the destruction of all desires.'
The two verses 186, 187 are ascribed to king
Mandhâtri, shortly before his death (Mél. Asiat.
VIII, p. 471; see also Gâtaka, vol. ii, p. 113).

188–192 These verses occur in Sanskrit in the
Prâtihâryasûtra, translated by Burnouf,
Introduction, pp. 162–189; see p. 186. Burnouf
translates rukkhaketyâni by 'arbres consacrés;'
properly, sacred shrines under or near a tree.
See also Gâtaka, vol. i, p. 97.

190 Buddha, Dharma, and Saṅgha are called the
Trisaraṇa (cf. Burnouf, Introd. p. 630). The four
holy truths are the four statements that there
is pain in this world, that the source of pain is
desire, that desire can be annihilated, that there is
a way (shown by Buddha) by which the annihil-
ation of all desires can be achieved, and freedom
be obtained. That way consists of eight parts.
(See Burnouf, Introduction, p. 630) The eightfold
way forms the subject of Chapter XVIII. (See also
Feer, Journal As. 1870, p. 418, and Chips from a
German Workshop, 2nd ed. vol. i, p. 251 seq.)

CHAPTER XV

198 The ailment here meant is moral rather than
physical. Cf. Mahâbh. XII, 9924, samprasânto
nirâmayah; 9925, yo sau prânântiko rogas tâm
trishnâm tyagatah sukham.

200 The words placed in the mouth of the king of
Videha, while his residence Mithilâ was in flames,
are curiously like our verse; cf. Mahâbh. XII,
9917,

Susukham vata gıvâmi yasya me nâsti kiñkana,
Mithilâyâm pradîptâyâm na me dahyati kiñkana.

'I live happily, indeed, for I have nothing; while
Mithilâ is in flames, nothing of mine is burning.'
Cf. Muir, Religious Sentiments, p. 106.

The âbhassara, i.e. âbhâsvara, 'the bright gods,'
are frequently mentioned. Cf. Burnouf, Introd.
p. 611.

201 This verse is ascribed to Buddha, when he heard
of the defeat of Agâtasatru by Prasenagit. It exists
in the Northern or Sanskrit and in the Southern
or Pâli texts, i.e. in the Avadânasataka, in the
Samyutta-nikâya. See Feer, Comptes Rendus,
1871, p. 44, and Journal As. 1880, p. 509. In the
Avadâna-sataka, the Sanskrit version is—

Gayo vairam prasavati, duhkham sete parâgitah,
Upasântah sukham sete hitvâ gayaparâgayam.

202 I take kali in the sense of an unlucky die which
makes a player lose his game. A real simile seems
wanted here, as in verse 251, where, for the
same reason, I translate graha by 'shark,' not by
'captivitas,' as Dr. Fausböll proposes. The same
scholar translates kali in our verse by 'peccatum.'

If there is any objection to translating kali in Pâli by 'unlucky die,' I should still prefer to take it in the sense of the age of depravity, or the demon of depravity. To judge from Abhidhânappadîpikâ, 1106, kali was used for parâgaya, i.e. loss at game, a losing throw, and occurs in that sense again in verse 252. The Chinese translation has, 'there is no distress (poison) worse than hate.' A similar verse occurs Mahâbh. Sântip. 175, v. 35.

'Body' for khandha is a free translation, but it is difficult to find any better rendering. The Chinese translation also has 'body.' According to the Buddhists each sentient being consists of five khandhas (skandha), or aggregates, the organized body (rûpakhandha) with its four internal capacities of sensation (vedanâ), perception (sañgñâ), conception (samskâra), knowledge (vigñâna). See Burnouf, Introd. pp. 589, 634; Lotus, p. 335.

203 Samskâra is the fourth of the five khandhas, but the commentator takes it here, as well as in verse 255, for the five khandhas together, in which case we can only translate it by 'body,' or 'elements of the body.' See also verse 278. Childers proposes 'organic life' (Notes on Dhammapada, p. 1). There are, however, other samskâras, which follow

immediately upon avidyâ, 'ignorance,' as second
in the series of the nidânas, or 'causes of
existence,' and these too might be called the
greatest pain, considering that they are the cause
of birth, which is the cause of all pain. Sometimes,
again, samskâra seems to have a different and less
technical meaning, being used in the sense of
conceptions, plans, desires, as, for instance, in
verse 368, where sankhârânam khayam is used
much like tamhâkhaya. Again, in his comment
on verse 75, Buddhaghosa says, upadhiviveko
sankhârasanganikam vinodeti; and again, upadhiviveko ka nirupadhînâm puggalânam visankhâra
gatânâm.

For a similar sentiment, see Stanislas Julien,
Les Avadânas, vol. i, p. 40, 'Le corps est la plus
grande source de souffrance,' &c. I should say
that the khandhas in verse 202 and the sankhâras
in verse 203 are nearly, if not quite, synonymous.
I should prefer to read gigakkhâ-paramâ as a
compound. Gigakkhâ, or as it is written in one
MS., digakkhâ (Sk. gighatsâ), means not only
'hunger,' but 'appetite, desire.'

204 Childers translates, 'the best kinsman is a man
you can trust.'

205 Cf. Suttanipâta, v. 256.

207 I should like to read sukho *ka* dhîrasamvâço.

CHAPTER XVI

214 See Beal, Catena, p. 200.

218 Ûrdhvamsrotas or uddhamsoto is the technical
name for one who has reached the world of
the Av*ri*has (Aviha), and is proceeding to that
of the Akanish*tha*s (Akani*ttha*). This is the last
stage before he reaches the formless world, the
Arûpadhâtu. (See Buddhaghosha's Parables,
p. 123; Burnouf, Introduction, p. 599.) Originally
ûrdhva*m*srotas may have been used in a less
technical sense, meaning one who swims against
the stream, and is not carried away by the vulgar
passions of the world.

CHAPTER XVII

221 'Name and form' is the translation of nâma-rûpa,
the ninth of the Buddhist Nidânas. It comprises

everything in the phenomenal world. Cf. Burnouf, Introduction, p. 501; see also Gogerly, Lecture on Buddhism, and Bigandet, The Life of Gaudama, p. 454.

223 Mahâbh. XII, 3550, asâdhu*m* sadhunâ *g*ayet. Cf. Ten *G*âtakas, ed. Fausböll, p. 5.

227 It appears from the commentary that porâ*n*am and a*gg*atanam are neuters, referring to what happened formerly and what happens to-day, and that they are not to be taken as adjectives referring to âsînam, &c. The commentator must have read atula instead of atulam, and he explains it as the name of a pupil whom Gautama addressed by that name (see note to verse 166). Others take atula in the sense of incomparable (Mahâbh. XIII, 1937), and in that case we ought to supply, with Professor Weber, some such word as 'saw' or 'saying.'

230 The Brahman worlds are higher than the Deva worlds as the Brahman is higher than a Deva; see Hardy, Manual, p. 25; Burnouf, Introduction, pp. 134, 184.

CHAPTER XVIII

235 Uyyoga seems to mean departure. See Buddhaghosa's commentary on verse 152, p. 319, l. 1; Fausböll, Five Gâtakas, p. 35.

236 'An island,' for a drowning man to save himself; (see verse 25.) It is well known that Dîpankara is the name of one of the former Buddhas, and it is also used as an appellative of the Buddha, but this name is derived from dîpo, 'a lamp,' and has nothing to do with dîpa, used metaphorically here and elsewhere in the sense of resting-place, shelter, or even Nirvâna; see Childers, s.v. dîpo.

239 This verse is the foundation of the thirty-fourth section of the Sûtra of the forty-two sections; see Beal, Catena, p. 201; Suttanipâta, v. 962.

241 On atidhonakârin, see Morris, J. P. T. S. 1887, p. 100.

244 Pakkhandin is identified by Dr. Fausböll with praskandin, one who jumps forward, insults, or, as Buddhaghosa explains it, one who meddles with other people's business, an interloper. At all events, it is a term of reproach, and, as it would seem, of theological reproach.

246 On the five principal commandments which
are recapitulated in verses 246 and 247, see
Buddhaghosha's Parables, p. 153.

248 Cf. Mahâbhârata XII, 4055, yeshâm vrittis ka
samyatâ. See also verse 307.

249 This verse has evidently regard to the feelings
of the Bhikshus or mendicants who receive
either much or little, and who are exhorted not
to be envious if others receive more than they
themselves. Several of the Parables illustrate this
feeling.

251 Dr. Fausböll translates gaho by 'captivitas,'
Dr. Weber by 'fetter.' I take it in the same sense as
grâha in Manu VI, 78; and Buddhaghosa does the
same, though he assigns to grâha a more general
meaning, viz. anything that seizes, whether an
evil spirit (yakkha), a serpent (agagara), or a
crocodile (kumbhîla).

Greed or thirst is represented as a river in Lalita-
vistara, ed. Calc. p. 482, trishnâ-nadî tivegâ
prasoshitâ me gñânasûryena, 'the wild river of
thirst is dried up by the sun of my knowledge.'

252 See Childers, Notes, p. 7; St. Matthew vii. 3.

253 As to âsava, 'appetite, passion,' see note to verse 39.

254 I have translated this verse very freely, and not in accordance with Buddhaghosa's commentary. Dr. Fausböll proposed to translate, 'No one who is outside the Buddhist community can walk through the air, but only a Samana;' and the same view is taken by Professor Weber, though he arrives at it by a different construction. Now it is perfectly true that the idea of magical powers (riddhi) which enable saints to walk through the air, &c., occurs in the Dhammapada, see v. 175, note. But the Dhammapada may contain earlier and later verses, and in that case our verse might be an early protest on the part of Buddha against the belief in such miraculous powers. We know how Buddha himself protested against his disciples being called upon to perform vulgar miracles. 'I command my disciples not to work miracles,' he said, 'but to hide their good deeds, and to show their sins' (Burnouf, Introd. p. 170). It would be in harmony with this sentiment if we translated our verse as I have done. As to bahira, I should take it in the sense of 'external,' as opposed to adhyâtmika, or 'internal;' and the meaning would be, 'a Samana is not a Samana by

outward acts, but by his heart.' D'Alwis translates
(p. 85): 'There is no footprint in the air; there
is not a Sama*n*a out of the pale of the Buddhist
community.'

Prapa*ñ*ka, which I have here translated by
'vanity,' seems to include the whole host of human
weaknesses; cf. v. 196, where it is explained by
ta*m*hâdi*tth*imânapapa*ñ*ka; in our verse by
ta*m*hâdisu papa*ñ*kesu: cf. Lalita-vistara, p. 564,
anâlaya*m* nishprapa*ñ*kam anutpâdam asambhavam
(dharma*k*akram). As to Tathâgata, a name of
Buddha, cf. Burnouf, Introd. p. 75.

255 Sa*n*khâra for sa*m*skâra; cf. note to verse 203.
Creature does not, as Mr. D'Alwis (p. 69)
supposes, involve the Christian conception of
creation. Buddhaghosa takes sa*n*khârâ as the five
skandhas.

CHAPTER XIX

259 Buddhaghosa here takes law (dhamma) in the
sense of the four great truths, see note to verse
190. Could dhamma*m* kâyena passati mean, 'he
observes the law in his acts, or sees the law with

his bodily eyes?' Hardly, if we compare expressions like dhamma*m* vipassato, v. 373.

265 This is a curious etymology, because it shows that at the time when this verse was written, the original meaning of srama*n*a had been forgotten. Srama*n*a meant originally, in the language of the Brahmans, a man who performed hard penances, from sram, 'to work hard,' &c. When it became the name of the Buddhist ascetics, the language had changed, and sramana was pronounced sama*n*a. Now there is another Sanskrit root, sam, 'to quiet,' which in Pâli becomes likewise sam, and from this root sam, 'to quiet,' and not from sram, 'to tire,' did the popular etymology of the day and the writer of our verse derive the title of the Buddhist priests. The original form srama*n*a became known to the Greeks as Σαρμαναι, that of sama*n*a as Σαμαναιοι; the former through Megasthenes, the latter through Bardesanes, 80–60 B.C. (See Lassen, Indische Alterthumskunde, II, 700.) The Chinese Shamen and the Tungusian Shamen do not come from the same source, though this has sometimes been doubted. See Schott, Über die doppelte Bedeutung des Wortes Schamane, in the Philosophical Transactions of the Berlin Academy, 1842, p. 463 seq.

266–270 The etymologies here given of the ordinary
titles of the followers of Buddha are entirely
fanciful, and are curious only as showing how the
people who spoke Pâli had lost the etymological
consciousness of their language. A Bhikshu is a
beggar, i.e. a Buddhist friar who has left his family
and lives entirely on alms. Muni is a sage, hence
Sâkya-muni, a name of Gautama. Muni comes from
man, 'to think,' and from muni comes mauna,
'silence.' Ariya, again, is the general name of those
who embrace a religious life. It meant originally
'respectable, noble.' In verse 270 it seems as if the
writer wished to guard against deriving ariya from
ari, 'enemy.' See note to verse 22.

272 See Childers, Notes, p. 7. Nekkhamana-sukham
is explained by the commentator as anâgami-
sukham, the happiness of one who can be born
again once only in the world of Brahma. The same
commentator takes Bhikkhu as a vocative. The
last line is obscure, and Fausböll with his usual
modesty adds, num recte alterum hemistichium
intellexerim docti videant. The text of the
commentary is so imperfect that in its present state
it cannot help us much. Following its indications,
however, Childers proposed an emendation,
Bhikkhu vissâsa*m* mâ âpâdi, lit. priest, enter

not into confidence. Bhikkhu may, of course,
be vocative or nominative. I formerly followed
Fausböll's conjecture, but I should now prefer
to take Dhikkhu as a nominative, referring it to
the person who is speaking, i.e. I or the Bhikshu
in general, has obtained confidence or peace of
mind, as soon as he has obtained the extinction
of passions. Âpâdi is here not a first, but a third
person. Kuhn, Pâli Grammatik, p. 109. Appatto
stands for âpatto, Sk. âpanno. See Kuhn, Pâli
Grammatik, p. 119. Athavâ, in v. 270, means or,
and corresponds to vâ; it can mean nothing else
here but what it means everywhere, whether in
Sanskrit or in Pâli.

CHAPTER XX

273 The eightfold or eight-membered way is the
technical term for the way by which Nirvâna is
attained. (See Burnouf, Lotus, p. 519.) This very
way constitutes the fourth of the Four Truths,
or the four words of truth, viz. Du*h*kha, 'pain;'
Samudaya, 'origin;' Nirodha, 'destruction;' Mârga,
'road.' (Lotus, p. 517.) See note to verse 178.

For another explanation of the Mârga, or 'way,' see Hardy, Eastern Monachism, p. 280.

274 The last line means, 'this following the true path is to confound Mâra,' i.e. the discomfiture of Mâra.

275 The salyas, 'arrows or thorns,' are the sokasalya, 'the arrows of grief.' Buddha himself is called mahâsalya-hartâ, 'the great remover of thorns.' (Lalita-vistara, p. 550; Mahâbh. XII, 5616.)

277 See v. 255. Nibbeda is sthâyibhâva.

278 See v. 203.

279 Dhamma stands evidently for sankhâra, and means the five khandha, i.e. what constitutes a living body.

281 Cf. Beal, Catena, p. 159.

282 Bhûri was rightly translated 'intelligentia' by Dr. Fausböll. Dr. Weber renders it by 'Gedeihen,' but the commentator distinctly explains it as 'vast knowledge,' and in the technical sense the word occurs after vidyâ and before medhâ, in the Lalita-vistara, p. 541.

283 A pun, vana meaning both 'lust' and 'forest.' See some mistaken remarks on this verse in D'Alwis, Nirvâna, p. 86, and some good remarks in Childers' Notes, p. 7.

285 Cf. Gâtaka, vol. i, p. 183.

286 Antarâya, according to the commentator, gîvitân-tarâya, means interitus, death, it does not mean here an obstacle only.

287 See notes to verse 47, Thiessen, Kisâgotamî, p. 11, and Mahâbh. XII, 9944, 6540. To clear is used in the sense of making clear or easy to enter, like our own to clear the way.

CHAPTER XXI

292 Cf. Beal, Catena, p. 264.

294, 295 These two verses are either meant to show that a truly holy man who, by accident, commits all these crimes is guiltless, or they refer to some particular event in Buddha's history. The commentator is so startled that he explains them allegorically. Mr. D'Alwis is very indignant that

I should have supposed Buddha capable of
pardoning parricide. 'Can it be believed,' he
writes, 'that a Teacher, who held life, even the
life of the minutest insect, nay, even a living tree,
in such high estimation as to prevent its wanton
destruction, has declared that the murder of a
Brâhmana, to whom he accorded reverence, along
with his own Sangha, was blameless?' D'Alwis,
Nirvâna, p. 88. Though something might be said
in reply, considering the antecedents of king
Agâtasatru, the patron of Buddha, and stories
such as that quoted by the commentator on the
Dhammapada (Beal, l.c. p. 150), or in Der Weise
und der Thor, p. 306, still these two verses are
startling, and I am not aware that Buddha has
himself drawn the conclusion, which has been
drawn by others, viz. that those who have reached
the highest Sambodhi, and are in fact no longer
themselves, are outside the domain of good and
bad, and beyond the reach of guilt. Verses like 39
and 412 admit of a different explanation. Still
our verses being miscellaneous extracts, might
possibly have been taken from a work in which
such an opinion was advanced, and I find that
Mr. Childers, no mean admirer of Buddha, was not
shocked by my explanation. 'In my judgment,'

he says, 'this verse is intended to express in a
forcible manner the Buddhist doctrine that the
Arhat cannot commit a serious sin,' 'na hanti, na
ka hanyate.' However, we have met before with
far-fetched puns in these verses, and it is not
impossible that the native commentators were
right after all in seeing some puns or riddles in
this verse. D'Alwis, following the commentary,
explains mother as lust, father as pride, the two
valiant kings as heretical systems, and the realm
as sensual pleasure, while veyyaggha is taken by
him for a place infested with the tigers of obstruc-
tion against final beatitude. Some confirmation of
this interpretation is supplied by a passage in the
third book of the Laṅkâvatâra-sûtra, as quoted by
Mr. Beal in his translation of the Dhammapada,
Introduction, p. 5. Here a stanza is quoted as
having been recited by Buddha, in explanation of
a similar startling utterance which he had made to
Mahâmati:

'Lust, or carnal desire, this is the Mother,
Ignorance, this is the Father,
The highest point of knowledge, this is Buddha,
All the klesas, these are the Rahats,
The five skandhas, these are the Priests;
To commit the five unpardonable sins

Is to destroy these five
And yet not suffer the pains of hell.'

The Laṅkâvatâra-sûtra was translated into
Chinese by Bodhiruki (508–511); when it was
written is doubtful. See also *Gâtaka*, vol. ii,
p. 263.

302 This verse is difficult, and I give my translation as
tentative only. Childers (Notes, p. 11) has removed
some, not all difficulties, and I have been chiefly
guided by the interpretation put on the verse by
the Chinese translator; see Beal, Dhammapada,
p. 137.

305 Vanânte, within the forest, according to a pun
pointed out before (v. 283), means both 'at the
end of a forest,' and 'at the end of desires.'

CHAPTER XXII

306 I translate niraya, 'the exit, the downward course,
the evil path,' by 'hell,' because the meaning
assigned to that ancient mythological name by
Christian writers comes so near to the Buddhist
idea of niraya, that it is difficult not to believe in

some actual contact between these two streams of thought. See also Mahâbh. XII, 7176. Cf. *Gâtaka*, vol. ii, p. 416; Suttanipâta, v. 660.

307, 308 These two verses are said to be taken from the Vinaya-pi*t*aka I, 4, 1; D'Alwis, Nirvâ*n*a, p. 29.

308 The charity of the land, i.e. the alms given, from a sense of religious duty, to every mendicant that asks for it.

309, 310 The four things mentioned in verse 309 seem to be repeated in verse 310. Therefore, apu*ññ*alâbha, 'demerit,' is the same in both: gatî pâpikâ must be niraya; da*n*da corresponds to nindâ, and ratî thokikâ explains the anikâmaseyya*m*. Buddhaghosa takes the same view of the meaning of anikâmaseyya, i.e. yathâ i*kkh*ati eva*m* seyyam alabhitvâ, ani*kkh*itam parittakam eva kâla*m* sey*y*am labhati, 'not obtaining the rest as he wishes it, he obtains it, as he does not wish it, for a short time only.'

313 As to raga meaning 'dust' and 'passion,' see Buddhaghosha's Parables, pp. 65, 66.

CHAPTER XXIII

320 The elephant is with the Buddhists the emblem of endurance and self-restraint. Thus Buddha himself is called Nâga, 'the Elephant' (Lal. Vist. p. 553), or Mahânâga, 'the great Elephant' (Lal. Vist. p. 553), and in one passage (Lal. Vist. p. 554) the reason of this name is given, by stating that Buddha was sudânta, 'well-tamed,' like an elephant. He descended from heaven in the form of an elephant to be born on earth. On titikkhisam, see Childers, s.v. titikkhati.

See also Manu VI, 47, ativâdâms titiksheta.

323 I read, as suggested by Dr. Fausböll, yath' attanâ sudantena danto dantena gakkhati (cf. verse 160). The India Office MS. reads na hi etehi thânehi gakkheya agatam disam, yath' attânam sudantena danto dantena gakkhati. As to thânehi instead of yânehi, see verse 224.

325 On nivâpa, see B.-R. Petersburg Dict. s.v.

326 Yoniso, i.e. yonisah, is rendered by Dr. Fausböll 'sapientiâ,' and this is the meaning ascribed to yoni by many Buddhist authorities. But

the reference to Hemakandra (ed. Boehtlingk
and Rieu, p. 281) shows clearly that it meant
'origin,' or 'cause.' Yoniso occurs frequently as
a mere adverb, meaning 'thoroughly, radically'
(Dhammapada, p. 359), and yoniso manasikâra
(Dhammapada, p. 110) means 'taking to heart' or
'minding thoroughly,' or, what is nearly the same,
'wisely.' In the Lalita-vistara, p. 41, the commentator has clearly mistaken yonisah, changing it
to ye niso, and explaining it by yamanisam,
whereas M. Foucaux has rightly translated it by
'depuis l'origine.' Professor Weber suspected in
yonisah a double entendre, but even grammar
would show that our author is innocent of it. In
Lalita-vistara, p. 544, l. 4, ayonisa occurs in the
sense of error.

327 Appamâdarata, not delighting in pamâda.

328, 329 Cf. Suttanipâta, vv. 44, 45.

332 The commentator throughout takes these words,
like matteyyatâ, &c., to signify, not the status of
a mother, or maternity, but reverence shown to a
mother.

CHAPTER XXIV

334 This is explained by a story in the Chinese
translation. Beal, Dhammapada, p. 148.

335 Bîra*n*a grass is the Andropogon muricatum, and the
scented root of it is called Usîra (cf. verse 337).

338 On Anusaya, i.e. Anusaya (Anlage), see
Wassiljew, Der Buddhismus, p. 240 seq.

339 The thirty-six channels, which are divided by the
commentator into eighteen external and eighteen
internal, are explained by Burnouf (Lotus, p. 649),
from a gloss of the *G*inaala*n*kâra: 'L'indication
précise des affections dont un Buddha acte
indépendant, affections qui sont au nombre de
dix-huit, nous est fourni par la glose d'un livre
appartenant aux Buddhistes de Ceylan,' &c.
Gray, however, takes them as the six organs of
sense, the six objects of sense, in relation (1) to
a desire for sensual pleasure, (2) to a desire for
existence, and (3) to a desire for non-existence.
Subhûti gives the right reading as manâpassavanâ;
cf. Childers, Notes, p. 12.

Vâhâ, which Dr. Fausböll translates by 'equi,'
should be vahâ, 'undae.' Cf. Suttanipâta, v. 1034.

344 This verse seems again full of puns, all connected
with the twofold meaning of vana, 'forest and
lust.' By replacing 'forest' by 'lust,' we may
translate: 'He who, when free from lust, gives
himself up to lust, who, when removed from lust
runs into lust, look at that man,' &c. Nibbana,
though with a short a, may be intended to
remind the hearer of Nibbâna. The right reading,
according to Childers, Notes, p. 8, is nibbanatho.

345 Apekhâ, apekshâ, 'care;' see Manu VI, 41, 49;
Suttanipâta, v. 37; and Gâtaka, vol. ii, p. 140.

346 Paribbag, i.e. parivrag; see Manu VI, 41.

347 The commentator explains the simile of the spider
as follows: 'As a spider, after having made its
thread-web, sits in the middle, and after killing
with a violent rush a butterfly or a fly which has
fallen in its circle, drinks its juice, returns, and
sits again in the same place, in the same manner
creatures who are given to passions, depraved
by hatred, and maddened by wrath, run along
the stream of thirst which they have made
themselves, and cannot cross it,' &c.

352 As to nirutti, and its technical meaning among the
     Buddhists, see Burnouf, Lotus, p. 841. Fausböll
     translates 'niruttis vocabulorum peritus,' which
     may be right, if we take nirutti in the sense of the
     language of the Scriptures. See note to verse 363.
     Could not sannipâta mean saṃhitâ or sannikarsha?
     Sannipâta occurs in the Sâkala-prâtisâkhya, but
     with a different meaning.

353 Cf. Suttanipâta, v. 210. The commentator explains
     that this verse was spoken by Buddha on his way
     to Bârânasî, in answer to Upaka, who had asked
     him who his teacher was, when Buddha asserted
     that he had no teacher. Childers accepts this
     explanation, s.v. uddigati. See also Lalita-vistara
     XXVI, ed. Calc. p. 526 seq., and read tenopaka
     gino hy aham.

354 The dhammadâna, or 'gift of the law,' is the
     technical term for instruction in the Buddhist
     religion. See Buddhaghosha's Parables, p. 160,
     where the story of the Sakkadevarâga is told, and
     where a free rendering of our verse is given.

358 'Vanity and vexation of spirit,' Ecclesiastes.

CHAPTER XXV

363 On artha and dharma, see Stanislas Julien, Les
Avadânas, I, 217, note: 'Les quatre connaissances
sont; 1° la connaissance du sens (artha); 2° la connaissance de la Loi (dharma); 3° la connaissance
des explications (niroukti); 4° la connaissance de
l'intelligence (prâtibhâna).'

364 The expression dhammârâmo, 'having his
garden or delight (Lustgarten) in the law,' is
well matched by the Brahmanic expression
ekârâma, i.e. nirdvandva (Mahâbh. XIII, 1930). Cf.
Suttanipâta, v. 326; Dhammapada, v. 32.

367 Nâmarûpa is here used again in its technical sense
of mind and body, neither of which, however, is
with the Buddhists âtman, or 'self.' Asat, 'what is
not,' may therefore mean the same as nâmarûpa,
or we may take it in the sense of what is no more,
as, for instance, the beauty or youth of the body,
the vigour of the mind, &c.

368 See Childers, Notes, p. 11, who translates, 'where
existence is no more;' but if we take saṅkhâra
in the plural, it may mean states of the mind,
or predispositions, inclinations, good, bad, or
indifferent. Verse 383 supports Childers' version.

370 Morris, J. P. T S. 1887, p. 116, takes uttaribhâv-
aye in the sense of to cultivate especially. Fausböll
translates removeat. The five are differently
explained by the commentator. See also Childers,
s.v. samyogana.

371 The swallowing of hot iron balls is considered
as a punishment in hell; see verse 308. Professor
Weber has perceived the right meaning of
bhavassu, which can only be bhâvayasva, but I
doubt whether the rest of his rendering is right,
for who would swallow an iron ball by accident?

372 Cf. Beal, Catena, p. 247.

375 Cf. Suttanipâta, v. 337.

381 See verse 368. D'Alwis translates, 'dissolution of
the sankhâras (elements of existence).'

CHAPTER XXVI

385 The exact meaning of the two shores is not quite clear, and the commentator who takes them in the sense of internal and external organs of sense, can hardly be right. See verse 86.

388 These would-be etymologies are again interesting as showing the decline of the etymological consciousness of the spoken language of India at the time when such etymologies became possible.
But in order to derive Brâhmana from vâh, it must have been pronounced bâhmano; vâh, 'to remove,' occurs frequently in the Buddhistical Sanskrit.
Cf. Lal. Vist. p. 551, l. 1; 553, l. 7. See note to verse 265.

390 I am afraid I have taken too much liberty with this verse. Dr. Fausböll translates, 'Non Brâhmanae hoc paulo melius, quando retentio fit mentis a jucundis.'

392 I have followed Childers, s.v. yo, in the translation of this verse.

393 Fausböll proposes to read gakkâ (gâtyâ). 'Both' in the first edition of my translation was a misprint for 'birth.'

394 I have not copied the language of the Bible more
than I was justified in. The words are abbhantaran
te gahanam, bâhiram parimaggasi, 'interna est
abyssus, externum mundas.' Cf. Gâtaka, vol. i,
p. 481.

395 The expression Kisan dhamanisanthatam is the
Sanskrit krisam dhamanîsantatam, the frequent
occurrence of which in the Mahâbhârata has been
pointed out by Boehtlingk, s.v. dhamani. It looks
more like a Brâhmanic than like a Buddhist
phrase.

396 From verse 396 to the first half of verse 423, the
text of the Dhammapada agrees with the text of
the Vasishtha-Bharadvâga-sûtra. These verses
are translated by D'Alwis in his Nirvâna, pp.
113–118, and again by Fausböll, Suttanipâta,
v. 620 seq.

    The text contains puns on Kiñkana, which means
'wealth,' but also 'attachment;' cf. Childers, s.v.

398 D'Alwis points out a double entendre in these
words. Nandhi may be either the strap that goes
round a drum, or enmity; varatta may be either
a thong or attachment; sandâna either chain or
scepticism; sahanakkamam either due order or all

[173]

its concomitants; paligha either obstacle or
ignorance.

399 The exact meaning of balâniṁ is difficult to find.
Does it mean, possessed of a strong army, or
facing a force, or leading a force?

405 On tasa and thâvara, see Childers, s.v., and
D'Alwis, Nirvâna, p. 115. On danda, 'the rod,' see
Hibbert Lectures, p. 355, note.

411 Akathaṅkathi is explained by Buddhaghosa as
meaning, 'free from doubt or hesitation.' He also
uses kathaṅkathâ in the sense of 'doubt' (verse
414). In the Kâvyâdarsa, III, 17, the commentator
explains akatham by kathârahitam, nirvivâdam,
which would mean, 'without a kathâ, a speech,
a story without contradiction, unconditionally.'
From our passage, however, it seems as if
kathaṅkathâ was a noun derived from
kathaṅkathayati, 'to say How, how?' so that
neither the first nor the second element had
anything to do with kath, 'to relate;' and in that
case akatham, too, ought to be taken in the sense
of 'without a Why.'

412 See verse 39. The distinction between good and
evil vanishes when a man has retired from the

world, and has ceased to act, longing only for deliverance.

418 Upadhi, if not used in a technical sense, is best translated by 'passions or affections.' Technically there are four upadhis or substrata, viz. the kandhas, kâma, 'desire,' kilesa, 'sin,' and kamma, 'work.' The Brâhmana may be called nirupadhi, as being free from desire, misery, and work and its consequences, but not yet of the kandhas, which end through death only. The commentator explains nirupadhi by nirupakkilesa, 'free from sin.' See Childers, s.v. nibbâna, p. 268 a.

419 Sugata is one of those many words in Buddhist literature which it is almost impossible to translate, because they have been taken in so many acceptations by the Buddhists themselves. Sugata etymologically means 'one who has fared well,' sugati means 'happiness and blessedness.' It is wrong to translate it literally by 'welcome,' for that in Sanskrit is svâgata; and we can hardly accept Dr. Eitel's statement (Handbook, p. 138) that sugata stands incorrectly for svâgata. Sugata is one of the not very numerous technical terms in Buddhism for which hitherto we know of no antecedents in earlier Brahmanism. It may have

been used in the sense of 'happy and blessed,'
but it never became a title, while in Buddhism it
has become, not only a title, but almost a proper
name of Buddha. The same applies to tathâgata,
lit. 'thus come,' but used in Sanskrit very much
like tathâvidha, in the sense of talis, while in
Buddhism it means a Buddha. There are of course
many interpretations of the word, and many
reasons are given why Buddhas should be called
Tathâgata (Burnouf, Introduction, p. 75, &c.).
Boehtlingk s.v. supposed that, because Buddha
had so many predicates, he was, for the sake of
brevity, called 'such a one as he really is.' I think
we may go a step further. Another word, tâdrisa,
meaning talis, becomes in Pâli, under the form of
tâdi, a name of Buddha's disciples, and afterwards
of Buddha himself. If applied to Buddha's
disciples, it may have meant originally 'such as
he,' i.e. his fellows; but when applied to Buddha
himself, it can only mean 'such a one,' i.e. 'so
great a man.' The Sanskrit mârsha is probably the
Pâli mâriso, which stands for mâdiso, Sk. mâdrisa,
'like me,' used in Pâli when a superior addresses
others as his equals, and afterwards changed into
a mere title of respect.

INDEX

The figures of this Index refer to the numbers of the verses.

WATKINS
1893

The story of Watkins began in 1893, when scholar of esotericism John Watkins founded our bookshop, inspired by the lament of his friend and teacher Madame Blavatsky that there was nowhere in London to buy books on mysticism, occultism or metaphysics. That moment marked the birth of Watkins, soon to become the publisher of many of the leading lights of spiritual literature, including Carl Jung, Rudolf Steiner, Alice Bailey and Chögyam Trungpa.

Today, the passion at Watkins Publishing for vigorous questioning is still resolute. Our stimulating and groundbreaking list ranges from ancient traditions and complementary medicine to the latest ideas about personal development, holistic wellbeing and consciousness exploration. We remain at the cutting edge, committed to publishing books that change lives.

DISCOVER MORE AT:
www.watkinspublishing.com

| Read our blog | Watch and listen to our authors in action | Sign up to our mailing list |

We celebrate conscious, passionate, wise and happy living.
Be part of that community by visiting

 /watkinspublishing   @watkinswisdom

 /watkinsbooks   @watkinswisdom